# Six New Testament Walks in Jerusalem

# Six New Testament Walks in Jerusalem

BY I. MARTIN

HARPER & ROW
*Publishers, San Francisco*

Cambridge, Hagerstown, New York, Philadelphia
London, Mexico City, São Paulo, Singapore, Sydney

PHOTOS BY Bob Grau, Jerusalem
DRAWINGS BY David Isaacs, Jerusalem

 For information address Harper & Row, Publishers, Inc., 10 East 53rd Street, New York, NY 10022. Published simultaneously in Canada by Fitzhenry & Whiteside, Limited, Toronto.

**Library of Congress Cataloging-in-Publication Data**

Martin, I.
Six New Testament Walks.

1. Jerusalem—Description—Tours. 2. Jesus Christ—Biography—Passion Week. 3. Bible. N.T. Gospels—Geography. I. Title.
DS109.M26 1986 225.9'1 85-45718
ISBN 0-06-065442-2

FIRST EDITION

Produced by Madison Publishing Associates

Designed by Stanley S. Drate/Folio Graphics Co. Inc.

86 87 88 89 90 10 9 8 7 6 5 4 3 2 1

*To:*
*Dr. James (Yaacov) Fleming,*
*Biblical Geographer*
*Director, Jerusalem Center for Biblical Studies*

# CONTENTS

# A WORD FROM THE AUTHOR

I begin all of my tour books of Jerusalem with the premise that all visitors to the city are literally COMING HOME. For all the monotheistic religions, this is really where it all began.

**The Text.** I have written the text in an informal, conversational manner almost as if I were your walking companion.

**The Walks.** You may have difficulty in completing all six walks during your stay in Jerusalem. You may not have six days in Jerusalem, and even if your time is not limited, your strength is. Moreover, there's only so much history you can absorb in a short time.

If you are pressed for time, consider doing the walks in the following order:

| WALKS | MORNING | LUNCH BREAK | AFTERNOON |
|---|---|---|---|
| Bethany/Mount of Olives | 1 | | 2 |
| Mount Zion/Model | 3 | | 4 |
| Temple Mount/Via Dolorosa | 5 | | 6 |

This doesn't mean, of course, that you should not feel free to do the walks in any sequence that is convenient to you. But to make sure you don't run into problems, please check very carefully the times of openings and closings of sites along each walk.

I thank you for coming to visit our Magic City of Jerusalem and trust that you will return here time and time again.

Jerusalem being home to everyone, let me say

Welcome home,<br>
I. M.

# INTRODUCTION: BACKGROUND FOR THE WALKS

In this book we are going to follow Jesus on his last week in Jerusalem. We meet him coming out of the Judean desert, heading for Bethany to see Lazarus his friend, who he was told is mortally ill. Then we follow him on his travels in and around Jerusalem during that last week of his life. And again we walk the paths he took on his way to Calvary.

I have tried to convey the times that Jesus lived in, for after all, the actions of every man are greatly influenced by his period. I hope I have been successful in presenting Jesus as a historical figure, founder of the religion of Christianity and inspiration for countless generations of men.

## THE SITES YOU WILL VISIT

For the most part I have chosen sites in and around Jerusalem that traditionally have been connected with Jesus' last week in Jerusalem. I have also included a few other sites that I feel you will enjoy visiting. They include a Crusader monastery in Bethany, a Tomb on the Mount of Olives dating from the time of the Prophets, and a huge water cistern at the Antonia Fortress from the time of the Maccabees (165 B.C.). I just couldn't resist showing them to you as we pass by.

Now for the big question.

### Are the Sites Authentic?

A good and fair question. In all truth, no one can say with absolute certainty that this or that is the exact spot where an event took place. So little written evidence has come down to us from two thousand years ago that we must rely heavily on tradition. But, as much as possible, I have placed an event at a traditional site or one that bears some resemblance to what is described in the written sources.

If you can agree with the above, then I am certain you will have a uniquely moving experience as you follow the route I have laid out for you.

## TELEPHONE NUMBERS

For further information here are the numbers for various sites along our Six Walks.

The Cenacle: 713-597
Church of All Nations: 283:264
Church at Bethpage: 284:352
Church of Dominus Flevit: 285:837
Church of the Holy Ascension: none
Church of the Holy Sepulcher: 284:213
Church of Pater Noster: 283:143
Church of Saint Lazarus at Bethany: 271-706
Convent of the Flagellation: 282:936
Convent of the Sisters of Sion: 282-445
David's Tomb: none
Garden Tomb: 283:402
Russian Church of Saint Mary Magdalene: 282:897
Saint Peter in Gallicantu Church: 283-332
Temple Mount: none

## PRACTICAL POINTS

In order that you get the most out of your walks I urge that you follow these suggestions.

**1. Summer: May 1 to October 31.**

- Our summer sun is very hot, and all walks should begin in the morning before 9 A.M. and earlier if possible.
- Drink two or three glasses of water or juice before starting out. This will prevent dehydration.
- You must—but absolutely *must*—wear a hat at all times.
- Carry a canteen with you.
- Wear sunglasses if you are beginning the tour in the afternoon.

**2. General tips.**

- Check your camera before starting out, and make sure you have extra film with you.
- If you wish to visit the churches on each walk, you must dress modestly. Shorts and tank tops are not permitted. We suggest that you carry a pair of jeans or trousers to slip on over your shorts if necessary. Ladies should take a scarf, so that they can cover their shoulders and arms when entering churches along the walks.
- Always carry either a candle or a small flashlight.
- Each walk takes between two and three hours.

**3. Visiting hours.**

- Many churches are closed to the public on Sundays, and during the week most churches are closed every afternoon from 12 to 2 P.M.
- We have listed the visiting times of each church along the walk, where it is appropriate.
- Telephone numbers for various sites are listed on the opposite page.

**4. Very important.**

- Jerusalem is a city of dynamic growth and change. This means that from time to time certain changes may appear that are not in the text. But in general you will have no difficulty.

**5. Transportation.**

- All the walks are a short taxi ride from almost every place in the city.
- When you get into a cab, make certain that the driver puts his meter on—you pay by the ride, never by the person.

| | |
|---|---|
| Taxi Rehavia | 224-444 |
| Taxi Israel | 222-333 |

A map of the city bus lines is available in the publication *Your Jerusalem,* a free copy of which you can pick up at all major hotels in West Jerusalem.

**6. Private cars.**

- It is very important that you check that all the doors are locked and that you have left nothing on the seats that could encourage vandalism.

**7. Carry your Bible with you.**

- Most of the relevant passages are quoted in the text (King James Version). However, you may prefer a different translation, and there will be many times when you will want to read directly from the Scriptures for yourself. I urge that you bring your Bible with you on all the walks.

## JERUSALEM SINCE JESUS' DAY

During your walks we will be making reference to two major periods in the history of Jerusalem when it was a great Christian capital. We will also be viewing archaeological remains from the early periods along the Walks.

EARLY CHRISTIAN PERIODS

| | | |
|---|---|---|
| Byzantine | (A.D. 324–638) | 314 years |
| Crusader | (A.D. 1099–1187) | 88 Years |

**Note: The arrow appearing on diagrams indicates north, which is not always toward the top.**

## THE SIZE OF JERUSALEM IN A.D. 30

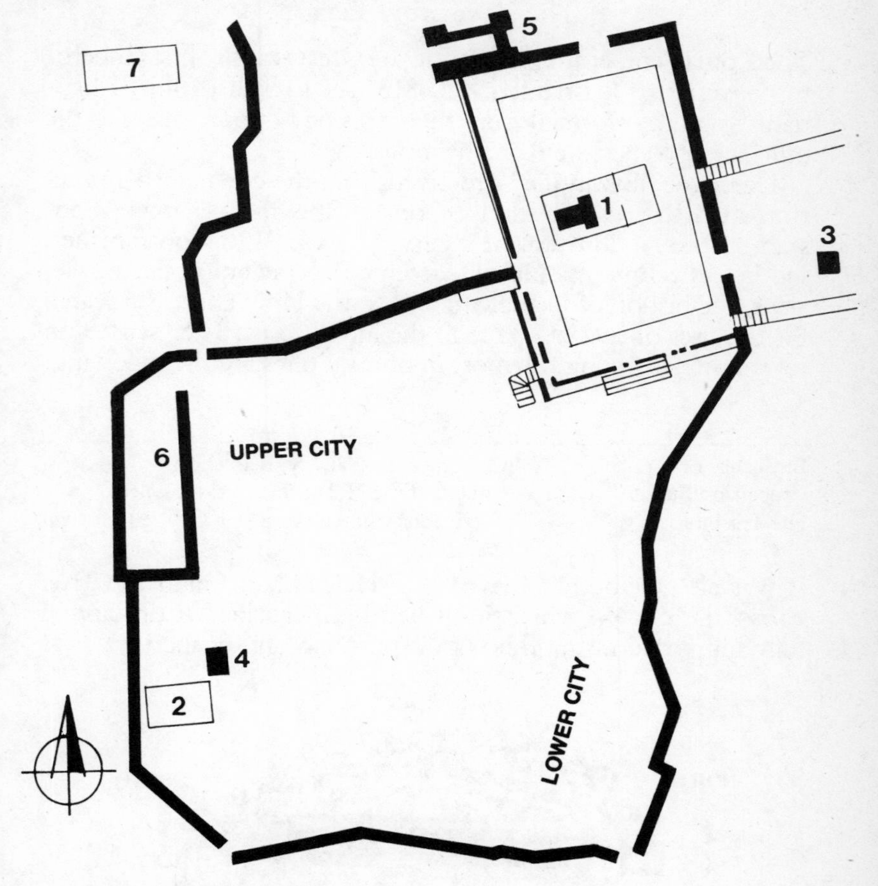


SCALE: 7/10 inch = 150 yards

| Number | Site | Event |
| --- | --- | --- |
| 1. | Temple | Preaching and cleansing |
| 2. | Cenacle | Last Supper |
| 3. | Garden of Gethsemane | Arrest |
| 4. | House of Caiaphas | Hearing before the high priest<br>Peter's Denial |
| 5. | Antonia Fortress | Held after sentencing (?) |
| 6. | King Herod's Palace | Pontius Pilate residence (?) |
| 7. | Golgotha | Crucifixion and Burial |

## The Byzantine Period

The Roman emperor Constantine the Great was the first emperor to convert to Christianity, A.D. 313. As a result of this, Christianity was transformed from the status of a minority sect to the official religion of the Roman empire.

The name "Byzantine" is derived from the city named Byzantium, which was rebuilt by Constantine and renamed Constantinople—"Constantine's City." In A.D. 326 Constantine's mother, the Empress Helena, accepted an invitation from Macarius, the bishop of Jerusalem, to visit the Holy Land and search for the sites of special events in the life of Jesus. They settled on several sites. Among the most important ones are the following:

| EVENT | SITE |
|---|---|
| Birthplace of Jesus | Church of the Nativity, Bethlehem |
| Crucifixion/Burial | Church of the Holy Sepulcher, Jerusalem |
| His Teachings | The Eleona Church, Mount of Olives, Jerusalem |

It was also devoutly believed that Helena had found the True Cross, the one on which Jesus had been crucified. Constantine fully supported his mother, both spiritually and financially.

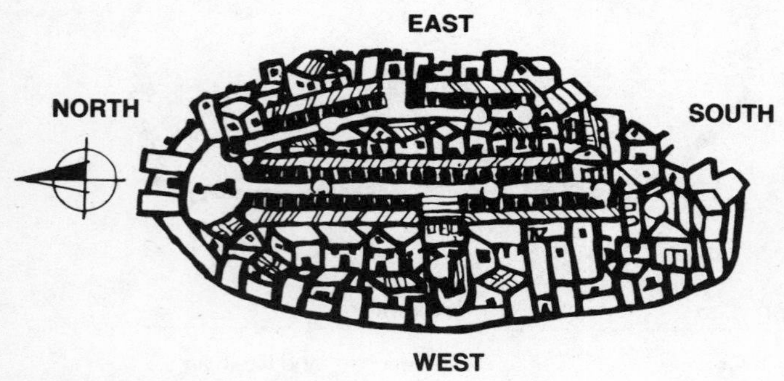


THE MADABA MAP

Pictured above is what is known as the Madaba Map. In 1884, a mosaic floor was discovered in a Byzantine church over the River

Jordan; its design was a map of the Holy Land. Included on the map was the only representation we have so far of how Jerusalem looked about fifty years before the Byzantines lost it to the Persians, in A.D. 614.

## The Persians Capture Jerusalem

In 614 the Persian army, after a twenty-day siege of the city, captured Jerusalem. The victors were ruthless and barbaric, slaughtering every Christian they came upon and carrying many thousands of others off to slavery in Persia. They burned and destroyed nearly every church in the Holy Land. Most Byzantine sites that are located today are covered with a thick layer of ash from the fires.

## Muslim Conquest

In A.D. 629 the Byzantines recaptured Jerusalem and brought the True Cross back into the city. However, seven years later, in 636, the Muslim invasion of Palestine began, and within two years they had the city under siege. A peaceful surrender was offered and accepted by the Muslims. This effectively ended Christian rule in Jerusalem for the next 461 years, until the Crusader conquest of the city.

## The First Crusade

Claremont, France, 1095, was the setting for the Church Council that was to launch the First Crusade. It was convened by Pope Urban II in order to "Return the merit and glory to the Christians, through a return to the Holy Land."

The armies enlisted under the banner of the Cross and the leadership of Godfrey of Bouillon and Bohemund of Otranto were composed of many undesirables—drunks, criminals, outcasts, those with nothing to lose—and as they marched across Europe on their way to the Holy Land, they killed, raped, and massacred many innocent people. But they defeated the Seljuk Turks at Dorylaeum (modern Eskesehir) on July 1, 1097, and took Antioch the following year. In June, 1099, they reached the walls of Jerusalem. After a forty-day siege and a day and a half of fierce battles to scale the walls of the Old City, the Crusaders broke through on Friday, July 15, 1099.

## Jerusalem Again a Capital City

After the destruction of the city by the Romans in A.D. 70, Jerusalem had been downgraded from a capital to a provincial town. For a thousand years, that's what it had remained. The Crusaders reinstated Jerusalem by designating it as their capital.

A massive and frantic building campaign got under way throughout the Holy Land almost immediately after their victory: castles, churches, hospices, monasteries, residences for the clergy, and many other types of buildings. Recent excavations have revealed the remains of countless Crusader edifices, whose remains we can see today.

## The Crusaders Lose Jerusalem

Although they built up the city, which indicates that they intended to stay for many generations, the Crusaders could not hold Jerusalem for long. On July 4, 1187, the sultan of Egypt, Salah-al-Din, known to the West as Saladin, decimated the main crusader army in a fierce battle at a place near the Sea of Galilee known as the Horns of Hattin. By September 20 of that same year, Saladin's army approached the walls of the Old City. Twelve days later the Crusaders surrendered. Saladin was a benevolent ruler. He granted clemency to all Christians and respected their church property.

## The Crusader Presence

Although they had lost control of Jerusalem, the Crusaders maintained cities along the Mediterranean coastline. Saladin couldn't overcome their naval power and finally signed a status-quo agreement with them. It left the coastline as far south as Jaffa to the Crusaders and also allowed pilgrims from all over the world to visit the holy Christian sites in Jerusalem. This arrangement lasted about a hundred years. But Jerusalem reverted again to a provincial city.

### A Brief Victory

For a ten-year period in the thirteenth century, Jerusalem was once again controlled by the Crusaders. But in 1244 the Mamluks, a powerful military class in Egypt, captured Jerusalem, and this ended Christian rule for almost seven centuries.

## THE TEMPLE AND THE TEMPLE MOUNT

I feel that, in order to understand Jesus' actions, we must know the times in which he lived. Overt political factors and current events did influence him, as we shall see during our Walks. But first I want to describe and explain the structure that dominated life in Jerusalem—and indeed all of the Holy Land—during the days when Jesus walked and taught in the city.

I used the following three sources for this study:

**The Talmud.** This collection of scholarly rabbinical writings provides us with the minutest detail regarding measurements and regulations that concerned the Temple. But one must bear in mind that it was written for future generations of Jews, who it was hoped would one day rebuild the great temple.

**Flavius Josephus.** Josephus was the major historian of this era and region. He was a Jew, a priest, and at one time a military leader of the northern part of Israel, who became a turncoat and went over to the Romans. His records are based on personal observation and have a strong reputation for accuracy.

**Archaeology.** The excavations by Prof. Benyamin Mazar and field archaeologist Meir ben Dov of the Hebrew University Department of Archaeology since 1968 have turned up much scientific evidence at the Southern Wall of the Mount to confirm Josephus' writings.

### Short History of the Temple Mount

Why did King Herod the Great choose to build his Holy Temple on this Mount? It wasn't just by chance. Herod was familiar with the long historical sanctity of this place, which goes back to the time of Abraham. The Mount is believed to be the place where God first tested Abraham's faith. Genesis 22:2:

> And he said, Take now thy son, thine only son Isaac, whom thou lovest, and get thee into the land of Moriah; and offer him there for a burnt offering upon one of the mountains which I will tell thee of.

Mount Moriah is traditionally the site we refer to today as the Temple Mount, a decision with which most scholars agree.

In the tenth century B.C., King David decided to build a temple to house the Holy Ark. He purchased a threshing floor (a large flat area of bedrock) which we believe is located on the Temple Mount. II Samuel 24:18 and 24:

> And God came that day to David and said unto him, Go up and rear an altar unto the Lord in the threshingfloor of Araunah the Jebusite.
>
> So David bought the threshingfloor for fifty shekels of silver.

With King Solomon, David's brilliant son, who reigned in Israel 973 to 933 B.C., we have a more direct reference to his having built the First Temple on the Temple Mount. II Chronicles 3:1:

> Then Solomon began to build the house of the Lord at Jerusalem in mount Moriah where the Lord appeared unto David his father, in the place that David had prepared in the threshingfloor of Ornan [Araunah] the Jebusite.

Solomon's Temple (the First Temple) was destroyed by the Babylonian ruler, Nebuchadnezzar, in 586 B.C., and the Jews were sent into exile at that time.

## The Second Temple

Due to the Temple Mount's long association with Abraham, David, and Solomon, it became the most holy place for Jews to worship and a natural site for King Herod the Great (73–4 B.C.) to build his Second Temple.

Mount Moriah had been known as the Temple Mount ever since King Solomon built his temple up here. Herod had to expand the

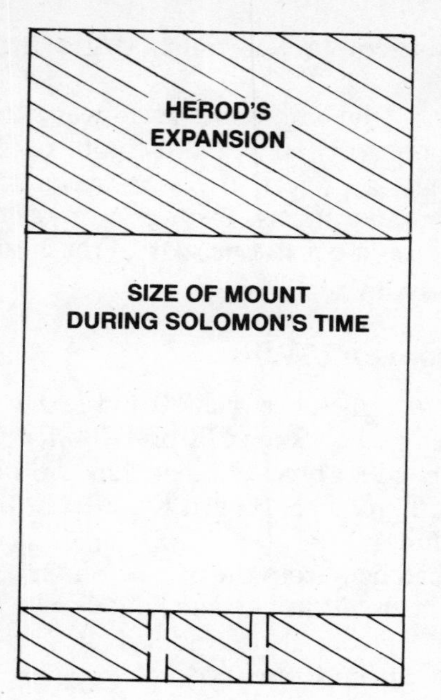

**EXPANSION OF THE TEMPLE MOUNT.**

Cross-hatching indicates section that Herod added.

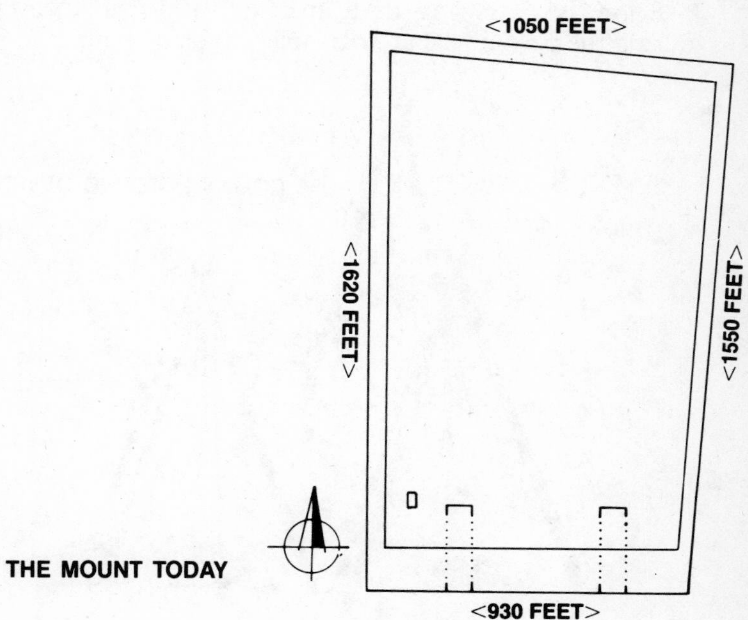


**THE MOUNT TODAY**

size of the Mount, since his temple was much larger than Solomon's.

The Temple Mount today is the same size as it was after Herod's expansion. It took about forty-six years to complete the full plan with all the buildings, a project involving about ten thousand workmen and a thousand priests. It covers an area of about forty acres, and in land mass it equals one sixth of the entire Old City. It was dedicated in 10 B.C.

## The Supporting Walls

The average stone in the walls weighed between 80 and 120 tons and the walls on each side averaged between 200 and 300 feet in height. The stones were quarried so precisely that they did not need to use cement between the courses. Given these facts, the question arises of how they built it.

One answer is that Herod had help from the premier engineers of the ancient world, the Romans. Although the king employed thousands of local people for the construction job, he nevertheless brought top engineers over from Rome.

Below is a drawing of Roman hoisting equipment in use during the period when the Temple was being built.

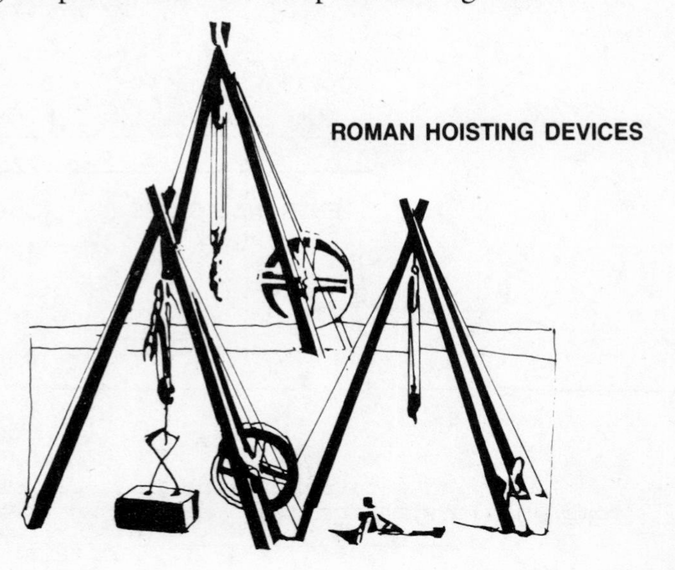

ROMAN HOISTING DEVICES

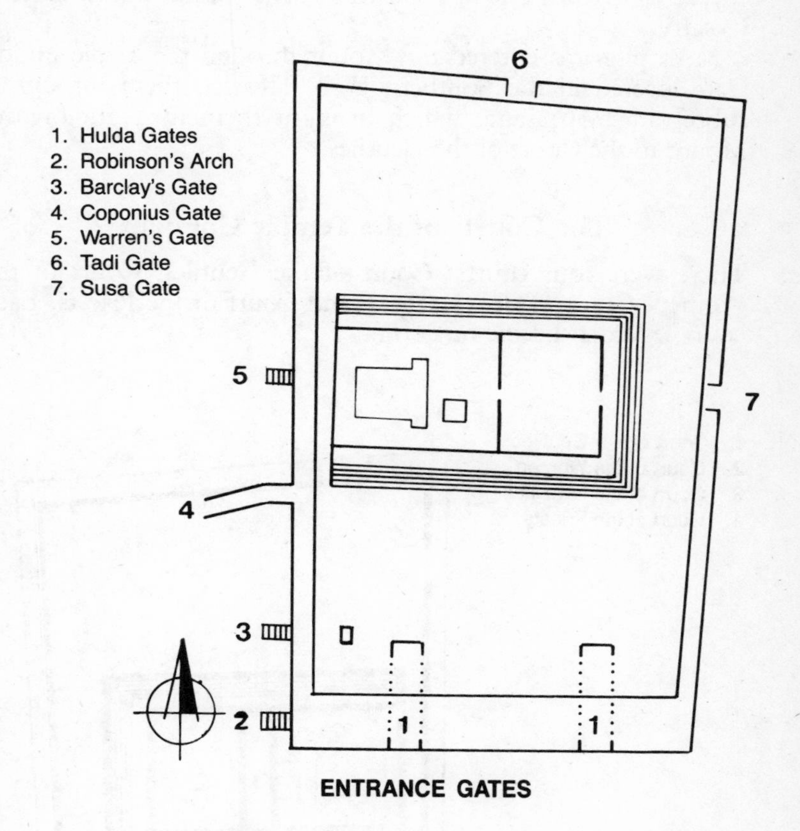


With the exception of sufferers from gonorrhea or leprosy, menstruating women, and people who did not take a ritual bath *(Mikvah)*, all pilgrims including non-Jews could go up on the Mount. However, Gentiles were barred from the Temple area.

The *Mikvah* was a ritual submersion in a pool to purify a pilgrim before he could enter the Temple grounds. Purification was required after sexual intercourse, after touching a dead animal, after menstruation, if one suffered from a discharge or flux of some kind, after contact with leprosy, venereal disease, or a corpse, and when one had shown evidence of having committed idolatry.

Most pilgrims entered the Mount through the Triple Hulda Gate located in the Southern Wall. This led them through a subterranean passage, which brought them up right on the Mount in the Court of the Gentiles.

## The Courts of the Temple Complex

There were four courts: Court of the Gentiles, Court of the Women, Court of the Israelites, and Court of the Priests. Each court served a specific function.

1. Court of the Gentiles
2. Court of the Women
3. Court of the Israelites
4. Court of the Priests

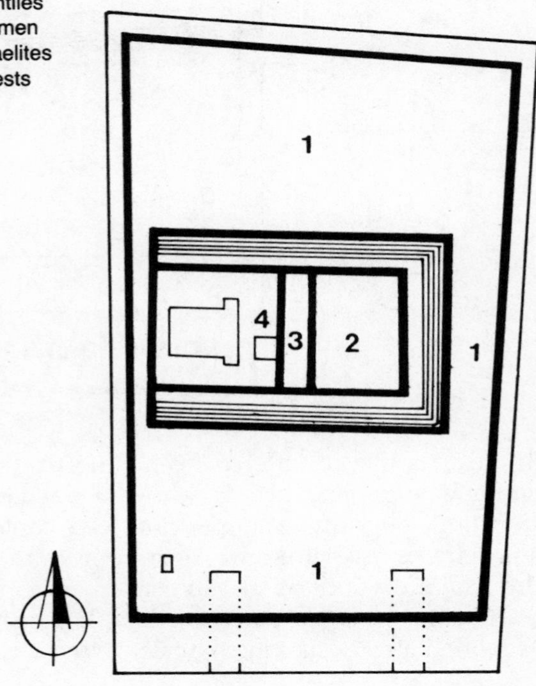

## The Court of the Gentiles

This was the largest court. Jews could continue on to the inner courts. Non-Jews were restricted to this one. Many non-Jews when in Jerusalem visited the Mount to see the beautiful Temple. (In Jerusalem today visitors of all faiths visit the Temple Mount to see the Dome of the Rock, a Muslim shrine.) A Talmudic tradition (*Baba Bathra* 4) states that

> He who has not seen the Temple of Israel has never in his life seen a beautiful structure.

## The Balustrade (Soreg)

The Balustrade was a low screened wall separating the inner courts from the Court of the Gentiles. Non-Jews were forbidden to come into any of the inner courts of the Temple. Warning signs in Greek and Latin were posted all around the Balustrade.

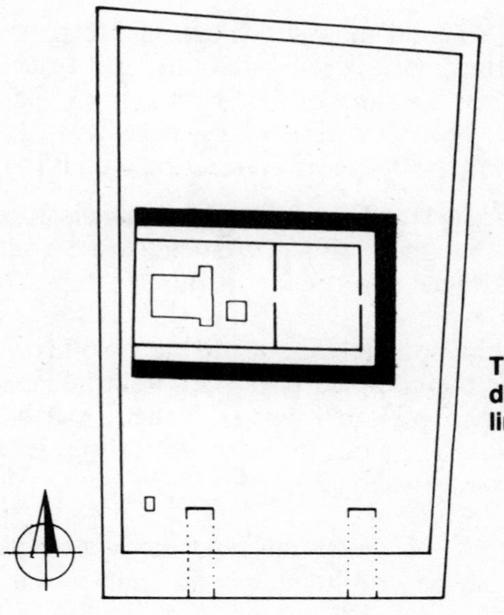

**The Balustrade is indicated by the black line.**

Two such warning signs have been found, one in 1871, one in 1935. The warning reads: "No foreigner is to enter within the balustrade enclosure around the temple area. Whoever is caught will have himself to blame for his death, which will follow."

FRAGMENT OF WARNING SIGN FROM THE BALUSTRADE

## The Beautiful Gate

Everyone wishing to enter the inner courts had to pass through this gate. Since the court it led out onto, the Court of the Women, was also the Treasury of the Temple, it proved an ideal spot for a beggar to solicit alms. That is why we recall the incident of Peter and the beggar in connection with it (page 180).

Although it was called the Court of the Women, all visitors to the Temple passed through it and also spent some time there. Women did not advance into the inner courts, except when they brought offerings, which were handed to the priests to sacrifice.

All communal functions relating to divine worship were conducted here. After the completion of the sacrificial rites on the Day of Atonement, the High Priest read the Torah before the people in this court. The pouring of water during the Feast of Tabernacles also took place here.

**The Treasury.** In this court the pilgrims would drop their donations to help support the Temple in thirteen trumpet-shaped

## PLAN OF THE TEMPLE COMPLEX AND INNER COURTS

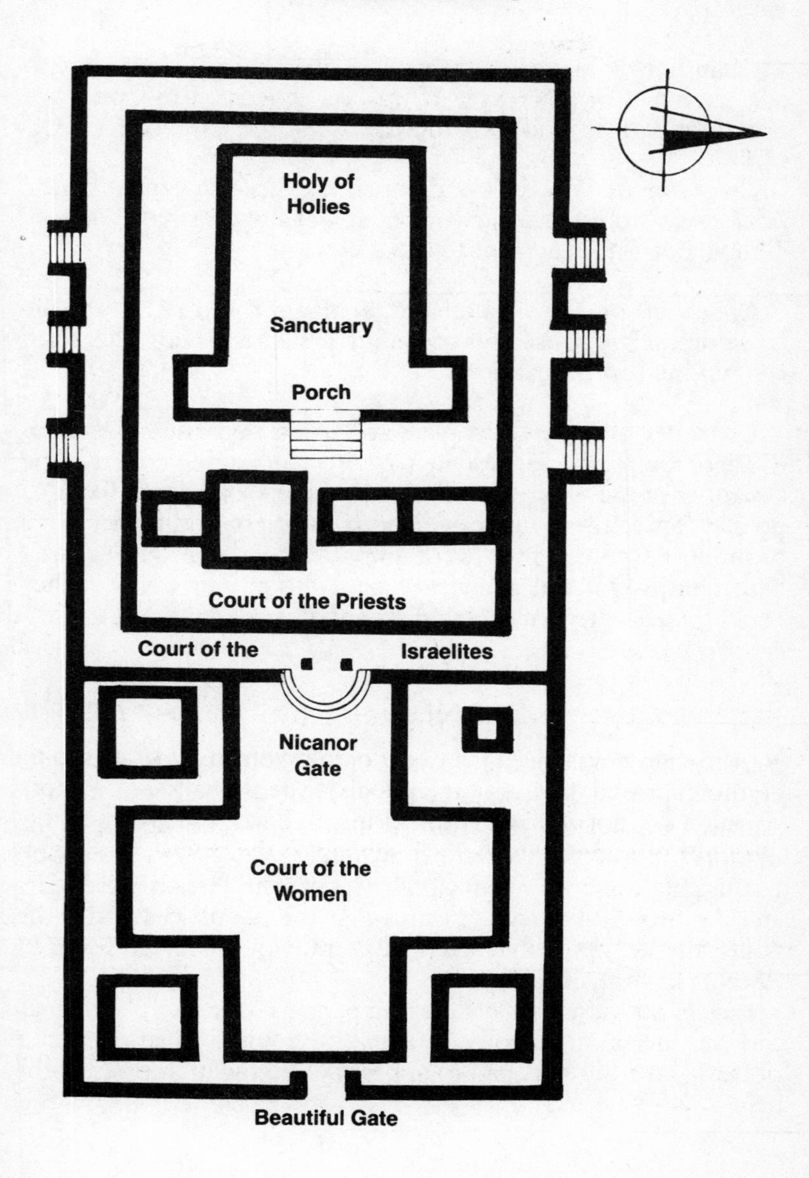

money boxes that were distributed around the courtyard. This is why we place the event of the Widow's Mite in this court (page 181).

**Chamber of Nazirites.** Every Jew was eligible at any time to take the vows of a Nazirite. It was a rededication to God. Paul was among those who took the vows.

**Chamber of Wood.** Wood which had been sanctified by the priests was stored in this chamber. It was used for repairs to the Temple buildings and for sacrificial fires.

**Chamber of Oil.** Oil played a major role in the Temple ceremonies. It was used for ordaining priests and was believed to contain medicinal qualities.

**Chamber of Lepers.** People with various skin diseases, including leprosy, were forbidden to enter the inner courts. The Chamber of the Lepers in the Court of the Women was for such people. There they were examined by a priest, and if they were pronounced cured, they went into the nearby *Mikvah* (ritual bath), and were then allowed to pass into an inner court. They could then also return to living among the general population.

## The Nicanor Gate

Between the Court of the Women and the inner courts was a gate crafted of bronze, brass, and copper. This was the Nicanor Gate, named for a wealthy Jew from Alexandria who donated it to the Temple. As you can see in the drawing, in front of and leading up to this gate was a wide semicircular set of stairs. Upon these stairs stood a group of priests (Levites). As the people came into the court, the Levites would serenade them with the fifteen songs of Ascents from the Psalms.

Lepers and other ritually unclean persons were also placed near this entrance in order to be cleansed. Also any woman suspected of being an adulteress had to appear before the high priest right here.

## The Court of the Israelites

Immediately inside the Nicanor Gate was the first of the inner courts, where men of the nonpriestly class (Israelites) assembled. It was the narrowest court of all, barely eighteen feet wide.

**Chamber of the Makers of Baked Cakes.** The priests who acted as bakers could prepare special cakes, which were considered ritually pure. They were used for ceremonial (shewbread) as well as for the priests' meals.

**Chamber of the Keepers of Priestly Vestments.** This was a storeroom for the ornate costumes worn by the priests, including the high priest, on festivals and holidays. One of the main things the Jews greatly resented was that the Romans confiscated all the vestments, and the Jews had to rent them back on the holidays.

**Chamber of the Hewn Stone.** Most scholars feel that this chamber was where the Jewish supreme court sat. It was called the Sanhedrin. They later moved to the Hulda Gate.

## The Court of the Priests

Only the priests were allowed in this court. Their job, aside from leading the daily prayers, was to conduct the ritual animal sacrifices for the pilgrims.

The pilgrims brought lambs, turtledoves, and pigeons and offered them to the priests for sacrifice to God and in this way atoned for their sins. Naturally the slaughtering of animals required certain practical and hygienic facilities. Those were as follows:

**Slaughter House.** There was a marble table where the animals were sacrificed. The table was surrounded by posts and hooks, which were there to hold and hoist the slain animals.

**The Ramp.** Both the ramp and the altar it led to were constructed of untrimmed stones "because iron is made to shorten man's life, whereas the altar was erected to lengthen man's years" as written in Middoth, 3.4, 226 c.

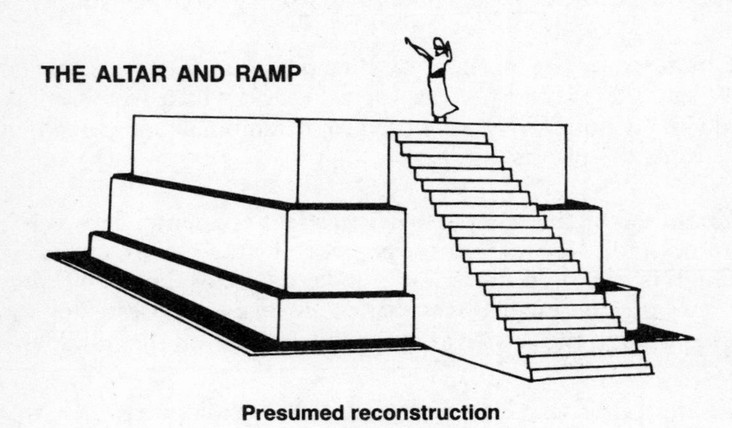


Presumed reconstruction

The altar stood in front of the Temple. It was approached from the south by the gently sloping ramp. Only priests were allowed on the altar.

**Chamber of the Hearth.** This was the off-duty resting place for the priests. There were various other chambers located in this court, running alongside the temple—Salt Chamber, Rinsing Chamber, Porwah Chamber, and the Chamber of Wood, all related to the sacrificial ceremony.

## The Temple Proper

Words alone are inadequate to describe the beauty and splendor of this magnificent building. Built of white marble and trimmed with gold, it was rectangular in shape and seventeen stories high. Its dimensions: 160 feet long, 160 feet high, and 110 feet wide.

MODEL OF THE SECOND TEMPLE, BUILT BY KING HEROD THE GREAT

**Steps.** Entrance to the Temple proper was by way of a flight of steps.

**Porch.** The porch contained four columns, two on either side of the entrance to the sanctuary. This facade is represented on Bar Kokhba coins (A.D. 132–135). Bar Kokhba was the leader of the Second Revolt of the Jews against the Romans.

**The Sanctuary.** The first hall facing the porch was called the Ulam. The second sanctuary was a rectangular structure, divided into two separate halls. The forward section was called the Holy *(Kodesh)* and the inner section the Holy of Holies *(Debir)*.

The entire face of the Temple was covered with gold, as were all the inner gates. Over the entrance hung very large grapevines of gold, some as tall as a man. There were no doors in the sanctuary itself. The room divisions were achieved by use of veils.

A Babylonian tapestry embroidered with blue, scarlet, and purple linen hung over the entrance. This mixture of materials was specifically chosen for its mystical connotations. It typifies the universe:

Scarlet—Fire
Fine Linen—Earth
Blue—Air
Purple—Sea

Worked into the tapestry was a panorama of the heavens, except for the signs of the Zodiac, which were woven into the design and represented the circle of the year.

There were seven lamps, representing the seven planets—that is, the seven heavenly bodies then regarded as planets: Sun, Moon, Mars, Mercury, Jupiter, Venus, and Saturn. Thirteen fragrant spices drawn from the land and sea represented all things that are from God and for God.

In the center stood an incense altar of gold. A gold-plated table for the shewbread (twelves loaves of consecrated unleavened bread presented to God every Sabbath) and a golden seven-branched candelabrum were placed inside as well.

## The Holy of Holies (Debir)

The Debir was a dark windowless thirty-three-foot cube. It was completely empty, as the Holy Ark given to Moses by God on Mount Sinai had disappeared sometime between Solomon's day and Herod's. The Debir was entered only once a year by the high priest, on the most Holy Day of Atonement.

The effect of this colossal building on the pilgrims was tremendous. Josephus tells us that its sides, overlaid with massive plates of gold, reflected the morning sun so brightly that anyone looking at it had to look away, dazzled. It was also described as appearing from a distance like a snow-covered mountain, since the parts not covered in gold were of the purest white marble. To prevent birds from perching on the roof and soiling the building sharp golden spikes were installed.

## The Temple Priests (Rabbis)

To qualify as a priest one had to be born into the family of a priest. There was one high priest, an appointed position.

Temple ritual required that the priests be divided into twenty divisions or groups. The Hebrew word for the act of dividing is *mishmarot*. Each division was from a different part of the country and conducted the rituals at the Temple for one week on a rotating basis.

משמרת ראשונה יהויריב מסרבי מרון
משמרת שניה ידעיה עמוק צפורים
משמרת שלישית חרים מפשטה
משמרת רביעית שערים עיתהלו
משמרת חמישית מלכיה בית לחם

**LISTING OF VARIOUS GROUPS OF PRIESTS**

The day began before dawn. The priests would take their ritual bath *(Mikvah)* and purify themselves. They then proceeded to the Chamber of the Hewn Stone located in the Court of the Israelites. Standing in a circle, they drew lots to decide their jobs for the day. The elder bade a priest go up to one of the towers surrounding the inner courts, and asked him if the light of dawn in the east had spread as far as Hebron. If the answer was in the affirmative, the priests then sacrificed a ewe lamb and prayed. Again lots were drawn to determine who would have the honor of working on the altar with the sacrifices. Then a priest sounded a *magrefa* (a gonglike musical instrument) which announced to the other priests and Levites the beginning of the morning song and communal sacrifices.

The lay worshippers assembled in the Court of the Israelites. The entire congregation was blessed by the officiating priests, then ceremonial wine was drunk and pancakes were prepared for

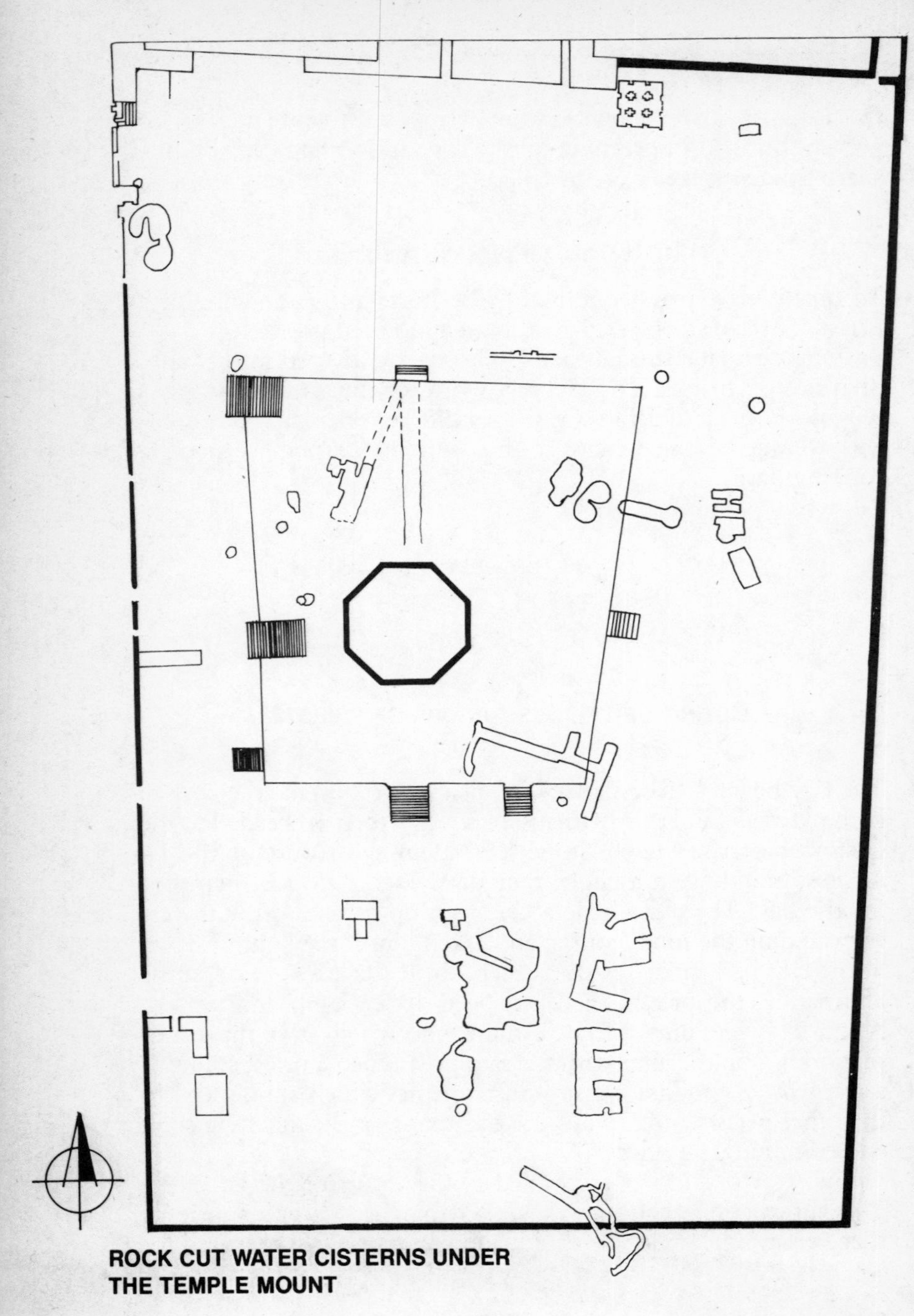

**ROCK CUT WATER CISTERNS UNDER THE TEMPLE MOUNT**

the priests. As the wine was poured, a signal was made to the Levites, and their band struck the cymbals and other priests blew silver trumpets. The Levites then recited the daily Psalm and read portions of the Law from the Holy Torah. After each verse, the trumpets were sounded. This daily ceremony lasted several hours each day.

After the completion of the services, the priests were kept very busy for the rest of the day since they had to sacrifice individual guilt or sin offerings that the pilgrims brought to them. The offerings took the form of a lamb, turtle doves, or even young pigeons (usually brought by a poor person); the pilgrim would make his offering, then relate his problems to the priest.

Slaughtering such a huge number of animals in an open courtyard required adequate provisions for waste removal. This was done by cutting channels into the floor of the Court of the Priests, where the slaughtering took place. These channels carried the waste outside the city walls.

The water supply for this sewage was provided by the twenty-six cisterns located below the Mount. These have a combined capacity of 12 million gallons of water. This water was also used for drinking purposes and for the ritual baths *(Mikvot)* along the Southern Wall. The drawing (opposite page) indicates the location of these cisterns.

## A Most Powerful Edifice

Thus the Temple played a large and powerful role in the life of the people during Jesus' time. Given that, it is understandable that very few people took seriously his prediction that the mighty building and its compound would be totally destroyed. Yet it came true a bare forty years later.

## ROUTE OF WALK 1

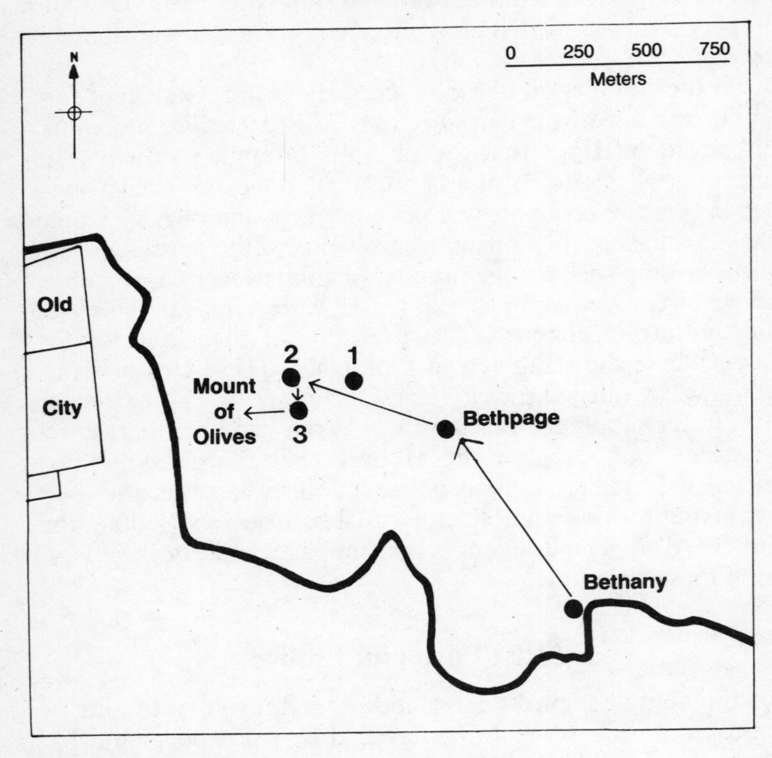


1. Russian Tower
2. Church of the Ascension
3. Pater Noster Church

# WALK 1

## *Approach to Jerusalem*

| EVENT | SITE |
|---|---|
| • Jesus meets Mary and Martha | New Church in Bethany |
| • Raising of Lazarus | Tomb of Lazarus |
| • The Triumphal Entry | Shrine at Bethpage |
| • The Ascension | Church of the Ascension |
| • Teachings on Mount of Olives | Pater Noster Church |
| • Jerusalem as Jesus Saw It | View from the Mount of Olives |

Today's tour goal is to capture the feeling of Jesus as he came out of the desert to the east of Jerusalem and made his way toward the city. On the way, he stopped off at Bethany to visit Martha and Mary and raise Lazarus from the dead, and we will recall this event, as well as the Ascension, the site of which lies on our route. Finally, we will get a first view of Jerusalem as it appeared to Jesus and reenact symbolically the Triumphal Entry, with which his last week opened.

## GETTING TO THE STARTING POINT

The starting point for today's walk is the town of Bethany. Bethany is known locally as El Azariya, meaning Lazarus. So if you are asking directions, try both names. *Important:* You must begin this walk no later than 9 A.M., since the church we are going to visit on our last stop closes at 11:45 A.M.

**By Taxi.** The last thing we want you to do is to spend your money on taxis when it is not necessary. But we do strongly urge that you take a cab out to Bethany. It's a ways out of town, and you will lose much touring time on the local bus. It's about a three dollar ride from the city of Jerusalem. Set the fee with the driver before you start out.

**By Bus from West Jerusalem.** Take the Egged bus No. 42 or 43 from the Central Bus Station on Jaffa Road. Ask the driver to let you off in Bethany or El Azariya. It's about a twenty minute ride from Jerusalem. Once you descend from the bus, cross the road and continue in the direction you were heading on the bus, and when you reach the little gift shop, take the path just past it to the church.

**By Bus from East Jerusalem.** Take the bus from the Central Bus Station in East Jerusalem, near the Damascus Gate. There is a sign on a post in the station that says in English "Bethany." Get off at Bethany (El Azariya), cross the road, and after a minute or so, you will reach a gift shop. Take the path just past it up to the church.

**By Car.** Drive to the Intercontinental Hotel on top of the Mount of Olives. Park in the hotel parking lot (no charge). Take a taxi from the hotel to Bethany. The walk today ends right up here near the Intercontinental Hotel, so your car will be waiting for you.

## BETHANY

Going to the RIGHT of the gift shop, walk past the garden, up the road toward the white stone church.

## The New Church of Saint Lazarus

The church is open daily, including Sunday, from 6 to 11:45 A.M. and 2 to 5 P.M. Its theme is the sadness of Death and the joy of Resurrection. It was designed by Italian architect A. Barluzzi and built between 1949 and 1953.

As you are coming up the path, notice the mosaic set into the front of the church. It is crafted from Venetian glass and shows Mary on the LEFT and Martha on the RIGHT. The center panel has a Latin inscription indicating that this church is dedicated to Lazarus. The two white doves represent sacrificial birds.

Continue up the hill and stop at the black iron gates on the LEFT. This is the entrance to the church. Part of the gate is painted red to display the symbol of the Franciscans, a large cross with four smaller crosses surrounding it. This symbolizes the responsibility of the Franciscans to carry the Gospel to the four corners of the earth.

Go through the gates into the courtyard below. The entrance to the church is on the LEFT through the

## Bronze Doors

The symbols on these doors all have special meanings. Endless Tresses indicate Eternity, Circles in High Relief are emblems of Life, and so on. On the left door, the Franciscan Cross symbolizes spreading the Gospel, and on the right door, Crossed Hands symbolize the Hands of Jesus and Saint Francis of Assisi, with the Stigmata.

Let's go inside the church, which is built over the traditional site of the house of Mary and Martha. The theme of this church is Salvation and Resurrection. This is reflected in the architecture and decorations.

## One Light Source

Notice that there are no windows. The only light enters through the dome in the center of the ceiling, which represents the Resurrection.

VIEW OF THE CHURCH OF SAINT LAZARUS

## The Earlier Church Remains

The first church on this site was built by the Byzantines.

**The Byzantine remains.** The two glass panels on the floor let us see the walls of the Byzantine church. Go over and take a look.

**The Crusader remains.** The Crusaders also built or rebuilt a church to Lazarus here. The panel in the floor up ahead shows the remains of the Crusader mosaic floor.

**Shape of a Cross.** The church was laid out in the form of a Greek cross, in which shaft and arms are of equal length.

**The left wall.** Walk over and look at the dedication plaque on the wall. It memorializes the visit of Pope Paul VI on January 4, 1964.

Now please walk over to the dome and stand under it.

## The Dome (Oculus)

Look up. The *oculus* (Latin for "eye"), or opening, invites you to follow the light rays up to heaven. In the forty-eight mosaics in the dome, the doves represent Eternity, Salvation, Resurrection, which can only come from God.

The Latin inscription running around the bottom of the dome is from John 11:25: "He that believeth in me, though he were dead, yet shall he live."

## Wall Mosaics

Now let's study these, using the altar as a starting point.

**Left wall.** Mary and Martha are speaking to Jesus in their home. Mary is at Jesus' feet and Martha at his side. Luke 10:38–39:

> Now it came to pass, as they went, that he entered into a certain village: and a certain woman, named Martha, received him into her house.
>
> And she had a sister called Mary, which also sat at Jesus' feet, and heard his word.

**THE DOME OF THE CHURCH OF SAINT LAZARUS AT BETHANY**

**Right wall.** We see a representation of the raising of Lazarus by Jesus. The stone that sealed the tomb has been moved away and we see Lazarus emerging dressed in his shroud. John 11:43–44:

> And when he thus had spoken, he cried with a loud voice, Lazarus, come forth.
>
> And he that was dead came forth, bound hand and foot with graveclothes.

**Above altar.** Jesus beseeches Martha to place her faith in him. John 11:25–27:

> Jesus said unto her, I am the resurrection, and the life: he that believeth in me though he were dead, yet shall he live.
>
> And whosoever liveth and believeth in me shall never die. Believest thou this?
>
> She saith unto him, Yea, Lord, I believe that thou are the Christ, the Son of God, which should come into the world.

After Jesus raised Lazarus, a turmoil erupted. Word of this miraculous feat spread very rapidly in Jerusalem. This was the

Messianic age, and the people in the city were awaiting the Messiah, who would give them both religious freedom and political freedom from the Roman occupiers.

Jesus needed time to think about this move, so he left Bethany and went a short way into the desert to a place called Ephraim. John 11:54–56:

> Jesus therefore walked no more openly among the Jews; but went thence unto a country near to the wilderness, into a city called Ephraim and there continued with his disciples.
>
> And the Jews' passover was nigh at hand: and many went out of the country up to Jerusalem before the passover to purify themselves.
>
> Then sought they for Jesus, and spake among themselves, as they stood in the temple, What think ye, that he will not come to the feast?

**Above entrance (rear wall).** The dinner after Jesus returned to Bethany from Ephraim. We see Jesus with his disciples, Martha and Mary, and Lazarus, and notice that the figure without the halo is Judas, who was to betray Jesus. Mary is anointing Jesus' head with precious oil and Judas objects. John 12:1–8:

> Then Jesus six days before the passover, came to Bethany, where Lazarus was which had been dead, whom he raised from the dead.
>
> There they made him a supper, and Martha served: but Lazarus was one of them that sat at the table with him.
>
> Then took Mary a pound of ointment of spikenard, very costly, and anointed the feet of Jesus, and wiped his feet with her hair: and the house was filled with the odour of the ointment.
>
> Then saith one of his disciples, Judas Iscariot, Simon's son, which should betray him,
>
> Why was not this ointment sold for three hundred pence and given to the poor?
>
> This he said, not that he cared for the poor; but because he was a thief, and had the bag, and bare what was put therein.
>
> Then said Jesus, Let her alone: against the day of my burying hath she kept this.
>
> For the poor always ye have with you; but me ye have not always.

Now walk up to the altar. The sculpture shows two angels beside the empty tomb of Jesus, with his shroud off to the side. The lovely green stone is Eilat stone, similar to the stone quarried in the southern Israel town of Eilat.

As you are heading for the exit, notice the small bronze plaques along the wall. They represent the fourteen Stations of the Cross that Jesus traveled on his way to Calvary. Look for them in the other church we will be visiting today. You might want to pick up a postcard or book as a souvenir. They are for sale in the vestment room on your LEFT as you exit.

As you step outside into the courtyard, you will see directly across from you, on the opposite wall, a bronze bust commemorating the visit to this church of Pope Paul VI. Note especially the blocked-off wall directly behind the bust of the pope. This was the original way of reaching the Tomb of Lazarus. It was sealed by the Muslims in the fourteenth century to prevent Christians from visiting the Tomb. In the early 1600s the Franciscans received permission to open up a new entrance to the Tomb, through which we will enter later today.

## Mosaic Floor in Courtyard

Look around at the several squares. Since the pillars are dated positively to the Crusader period and the tiles are set right into the base of the columns, this is archaeological proof that the floor was laid sometime between 1099 and 1187, when the Crusaders controlled the city.

## The Crusader Monastery

The remains you see in this courtyard and beyond are part of a twelfth-century Crusader Monastery and church that were destroyed. To your LEFT at the rear are three doors. Enter the one on the RIGHT. If it is locked, ask the friar in the church please to open it for you.

FLASHLIGHT ON.

Once inside, you will find clean bathrooms on the LEFT. Go through the door on the RIGHT. There is a LIGHT SWITCH just before you enter the door. Turn it on (and be sure to return here when you finish this site and turn it off). The first major piece you see is the large olive press.

COURTYARD OF CRUSADER MONASTERY

The first question you should ask is "Where were the olive groves?" You will soon see the groves. This huge press tells us how the monks supported the monastery, which is on the main road to Jerusalem: They sold olive oil, which had religious uses as well as culinary ones.

The olives with their pits were placed on the lower stone, and then a stone above was lowered and turned, crushing the pits and releasing the oil, which was then allowed to run down an underground pipe into a storage vat. The pulp could be squeezed for the last ounce of the oil, and that was the purpose of the huge wooden fork and corkscrew.

**Corkscrew.** The pulp was placed in baskets and put under the corkscrew. This was lowered and turned into the pulp, squeezing out the remainder of the oil. Now let's go and see the storage vat in the next room.

**The Storage Vat.** This is where the oil was stored and refined. Walk up a few steps onto the platform. Notice that the vat has

LARGE OLIVE PRESS

STORAGE VAT

CORKSCREW

signs of having been plastered. That's one way archaeologists can ascertain whether a container held dry or, as in this case, liquid contents.

## The Rest of the Building

Take the stairway on the right, leading up. As you make the first turn on the stairway, look down to your LEFT and study the original drainpipe. When you reach the second floor, you will see scattered on the floor some remains of the stonework of the Crusaders.

Walk to the end of this room and look down into the small inner courtyard. The reconstructed arch you see indicates that this was an enclosed courtyard in Crusader times. As you come back into the room, look at the marks of the severe burning on the ceiling. This tells us that those who destroyed it burned it.

Now let's go down below into the courtyard we just looked into. Return the same way you came, and exit from the door just past the vat on the left. Before you enter the courtyard, notice the lovely remains of the 800-year-old Crusader mosaic floor. Look for other remains of floors in the courtyard along the walls. To provide visitors with seats, the Crusaders set out large carved blocks of stone as benches. (They look to me like modern furniture.) Walking ahead, you will reach the black iron-grilled cistern. The water was centrally located for easy access to everyone living here.

We suggest that now is a good time to make sure the lights you turned on are shut off. Thanks.

We are now going to leave the church area and go to Momma's House. Leave the courtyard by going back up the stairs and out through the black iron gate. LEFT up the hill. A few steps ahead on the opposite side of the road on the RIGHT is a courtyard with a house set back a little bit. This is

## Momma's House

We are going inside to visit with Momma, to give you an impression of what living style was like in one of the ancient houses in the town of Bethany during Jesus' lifetime. Momma's house is only about six hundred years old and thus does not date to Jesus' day, but her style of living is pretty similar.

Nine persons live in this one-room house, all Christian Arabs. Momma's grandchild is named Jimmy Carter in honor of the visit of former President Jimmy Carter to Bethany. Another grandson is named Jesus, and her youngest son is Lazarus.

Most functions are carried out in the courtyard, including cooking over a charcoal brazier and eating. Bathroom facilities are also outside the house. The one room inside is used for sleeping.

Note especially

- the thickness of the walls;
- niches built into the walls for storage;
- the ancient floor of beaten earth;
- the large wooden closet, which is Momma's pantry;
- the niche on the right for schoolbooks;
- clothing hung on the wall hooks.

You might ask, How do nine people sleep in this one small room? A good question, and Momma has a good answer. Notice

**MOMMA, A CHRISTIAN ARAB**

that over Momma's bed, the one bed in the room, there are several quilts and blankets. She lays out straw matting on the cement floor, then puts blankets and quilts over that.

When leaving, it is customary to give Momma a small gratuity.

After you leave Momma's house, turn RIGHT up the hill, and you will see a large black sign on the opposite side of the road announcing that this is the entrance to

## The Tomb of Lazarus

DUCK your head upon entering; it's a very low entrance. Before you is a set of twenty-four steps. If you are entering after rain, be extra careful, for the limestone steps become very slippery. Please use the hand rail both going down and coming up.

The past two thousand years have caused the Tomb to suffer heavy erosion, and it is hardly recognizable today. What is important is that when you reach the bottom of the staircase, you are standing where the early Christians remembered the Tomb of Lazarus. This location is accepted by most scholars, and we have numerous reports of early Christian pilgrims who venerated this site.

The actual tomb itself is down three more steps and through a little tunnel. It is a wonderful place to read the story of Lazarus. John 11:31–41:

> The Jews then which were with her in the house, and comforted her, when they saw Mary, that she rose up hastily and went out, followed her, saying, She goeth unto the grave to weep there.
>
> Then when Mary was come where Jesus was, and saw him, she fell down at his feet, saying unto him, Lord if thou hadst been here, my brother had not died.
>
> When Jesus therefore saw her weeping and the Jews also weeping which came with her, he groaned in the spirit, and was troubled.
>
> And said, Where have ye laid him? They said unto him, Lord come and see.
>
> Jesus wept.
>
> Then said the Jews, Behold, how he loved him!

**ENTRANCE TO LAZARUS' TOMB**

And some of them said, Could not this man, which opened the eyes of the blind, have caused that even this man should not have died?

Jesus therefore, again groaning in himself, cometh to the grave. It was a cave, and a stone lay upon it.

Jesus said, Take ye away the stone. Martha, the sister of him that was dead, saith unto him, Lord, by this time he stinketh: for he hath been dead four days.

Jesus saith unto her, Said I not unto thee, that if thou wouldest believe, thou shouldst see the glory of God?

Then they took away the stone from the place where the dead was laid. And Jesus lifted up his eyes, and said, Father, I thank thee that thou hast heard me.

> And I know that thou hearest me always: but because of the people who stand by I said it, that they may believe that thou has sent me.
>
> And when he thus had spoken, he cried with a loud voice, Lazarus, come forth.
>
> And he that was dead came forth, bound hand and foot with graveclothes, and his face was bound about with a napkin. Jesus saith unto them, Loose him and let him go.

Go back up the stairs when you are ready and remember to DUCK your head as you go out the exit.

Turn LEFT, up the hill. There is a clean bathroom just past the souvenir shop across the road. The next rest stop is about twenty minutes away.

## BETHPAGE

For the next twenty minutes or so, you will be walking on a path that could have very well have existed in Jesus' time. It is the natural path to Bethpage from Bethany. As you go up the hill, the remains you see on your LEFT side are from the same Crusader Monastery we visited earlier. It overlooks the main road from Jericho to Jerusalem and served both as a defensive fortress and as a place for pilgrims to rest and purchase supplies before completing the journey to Jerusalem.

The white church up ahead on your LEFT is Greek Orthodox. We can't visit today. It is only opened once a year on the Greek Easter. When you reach the first dirt path on the RIGHT, turn RIGHT. There should be a low gray wall on your right. Look at the olive trees behind the wall. This is the orchard from which the monastery obtained its olives.

Walk straight down the path, and in a minute or two you will reach

### Four Caves

In front of you in the bedrock are the entrances. The cave farthest to the LEFT shows how some of the people of Bethany lived in Jesus' day. What we find particularly interesting is the cave on the

FAR RIGHT with the wooden door and window. This was for many years the home of the family who have since built and now occupy the beautiful white house next door. The cave is now used for their garbage.

Continue in the same direction you were headed, and at the fork bear LEFT. You will be passing almond and fig trees along this walk.

## Not Too Much to See

Yes, there are very few "sights" along this Biblical path to Bethpage. And perhaps that's a good thing, for it allows the visitor time to think about what Jesus and his disciples felt as they completed the last leg of their final journey to Jerusalem, which ended at Calvary.

In less than ten minutes you will see a very tall bell tower dominating the skyline above a line of trees. This is

## The Tower of Ascension

It is also called the Russian Tower, for this property is under the care of the White Russian church. It was built in 1870–1880, and it is maintained today by elderly nuns. It is six stories high and contains 214 steps. Tradition has it that, on the southeast corner of where the church now stands, the Virgin stood at the time of the Ascension.

An interesting story concerns the bell up in the tower. Under Turkish law it was forbidden to build a structure higher than any Muslim building. Therefore when the huge bell arrived from Russia at the port of Jaffa, the Muslim porters refused to unload it or carry it to Jerusalem. Legend has it that the sisters then brought it to Jerusalem themselves, probably loaded onto a cart.

You can see the Mediterranean sea along the coast of Tel Aviv from the top of the tower. Unfortunately it is not open to the public, since the nuns find it difficult to manage visitors.

When you reach the paved road at the end of this path, you are going to get your first view of Jerusalem.

THE TOWER
OF ASCENSION

Look straight ahead and to the LEFT. This is the Mount of Olives, which contains the oldest known Jewish cemetery in the world and dates back to Jesus' time. Topography changes very little over the centuries, which means that Jesus and his disciples had their first view of the city from a spot similar to this. Isn't the view breathtaking? Take a few steps up the hill, and you have arrived at

## The Church at Bethpage

The church at Bethpage is open daily, including Sundays, from October 1 to March 31 from 7 to 11:45 A.M. and 2 to 4:30 P.M., from April 1 to September 30, 7 to 11:45 A.M. and 2 to 5:30 P.M.

Reach inside the gate, and pull the cord. The bell on the RIGHT side will summon the gatekeeper. There is no official entry fee, but it is customary to offer him a small gratuity. The name "Bethpage" means "unripe juiceless fig." This has led many people to identify this site with the Fig Tree Parable. Mark 11:13–14:

And seeing a fig tree afar off, having leaves, he came, if haply he might find anything thereon; and when he came to it, he found nothing but leaves; for the time was not yet.

And Jesus answered and said unto it, No man eat fruit of thee hereafter for ever. And his disciples heard it.

FIG LEAF

Notice the fig and palm trees on this property. Before going inside the church, note the symbol above the doorway, which indicates that this church is maintained by the Franciscan order. Before entering the church you might want to read the English translation of the plaque on the wall at the entrance.

Inside the church, sit down and take a short rest while you meditate on the theme around which the church was built and dedicated:

## The Triumphal Entry

The church commemorates the arrival of Jesus and His disciples at Bethpage and their securing a donkey, on which he is to enter

Jerusalem. Why do you think that Jesus chose a donkey to ride when he entered the city? There is a possible answer in Zechariah 9:9.

> Rejoice greatly, O daughter of Zion; shout, O daughter of Jerusalem: behold thy King [Messiah] cometh unto thee: he is just, and having salvation: lowly, and riding upon an ass, and upon a colt the foal of an ass.

Pilgrims following the route of Jesus' Triumphal Entry on Palm Sunday usually walk from Bethany to Saint Stephen's Gate (Lion's Gate). They pass through the gate and from there proceed to Saint Anne's Church, to the RIGHT of the gate.

The symbol of Palm Sunday and the Triumphal Entry is of course the Palm Branch. It was more than just a coincidence that they chose it.

The Palm Branch has long been and still is a symbol of Jewish independence. We find it on Hasmonean (Maccabee) coins dating from 165 B.C. At that time the Jews fought and won their independence from the Greeks. We also see it used today as a symbol of the Israeli army. In Jesus' day the Jews were struggling against the Romans for their independence. It is logical to assume that the people, by waving palm branches as Jesus approached, were making a political statement against Roman occupation.

A HASMONEAN COIN

The present church was built in 1883 over the ruins of an original Crusader church. Let's explore it. Walk over to the high stone on the LEFT side of the church, enclosed by a black railing. This is called the

## The Stele (Mounting Stone)

The church was built around this stone, accidentally located in 1876. It has been venerated since the Crusader pilgrims first came

**THE MOUNTING STONE**

upon it. They believed it was the stone that Jesus placed his foot upon when he mounted the donkey.

The paintings on the stone date from the Crusader period, but in 1950 the outlines were touched up a bit; this is indicated by the brown lines you see. The paintings were preserved as they looked when the stone was first discovered in 1876; it had been buried for many centuries. Examine the paintings, orienting yourself by facing the altar:

**Side 1.** Martha meeting Jesus as he arrives from the desert. (It was once a popular belief that Bethpage and not Bethany was where Martha met Jesus.)

**Side 2.** Jesus watching Lazarus emerge from his tomb.

**Side 3.** The townspeople collecting palms and spreading their garments for Jesus to ride over.

**Side 4 (Mirror Image).** Two of Jesus' disciples getting the donkey for Jesus and some of the townspeople looking on.

## The Wall Frescoes (Paintings)

Beginning in the LEFT hand corner as you face the altar, here are the subjects of these wall paintings:

1. Simon Peter inside the gates of Bethpage, taking the donkey.
2. The resurrected Lazarus with his sisters, Mary and Martha.
3. Trumpets announcing the beginning of the procession.
4. Sacrificial doves of peace.
5. Outside the city gates of Bethpage, heading for Jerusalem.
6. The disciples carrying branches.
7. A young boy up in the tree collecting olive branches.
8. Woman carrying palm branches.
9. Roman soldiers guarding the entrance to Jerusalem.
10. Three pharisees with a sign, illustrating John 12:19: "Behold, the world has gone after him."

Now turn your attention to the altar, above which is

## The Large Mural

We see Jesus on his donkey on the way to Jerusalem. People are spreading their cloaks for him to pass over. On the LEFT side of

MURAL OF THE TRIUMPHAL ENTRY

the painting, we see that palm branches have been raised in an arch, for Jesus to pass under.

Notice the numbered plaques around the walls of this church. They represent the fourteen Stations of the Cross.

Now we are going to visit a tomb with a stone-seal entrance from Jesus' day.

## The Round Stone Door

One particular type of tomb was typical of New Testament times. This was a rock-cut cave. In order to keep wild animals out, men fashioned a flat round stone and rolled it across the entrance.

You will recall that Joseph of Arimathaea who was a disciple of Jesus asked for the body so he could bury it. Matthew: 27:58–60:

> He [Joseph] went to Pilate, and begged the body of Jesus. Then Pilate commanded the body to be delivered.
>
> And when Joseph had taken the body, he wrapped it in a clean linen cloth.
>
> And laid it in his own new tomb, which he had hewn out in the rock: and he rolled a great stone to the door of the sepulcher, and departed.

ROCK-CUT TOMB WITH STONE DOOR

When you leave the church, find the guard. He doesn't speak much English, but if you say the word "Tomb," he will understand you. Since you wouldn't be able to find it without his help, offer him another small gratuity. He will take you around the back of the church on the LEFT side and through a gate. Once you are walking down a sloping path, you will pass a small flat-roofed building with several doors. Continue ahead and notice, on the RIGHT, an outcropping of natural rock. Walk to the third hole in the rock and look in. Yes, that's it. If you have your flashlight, you might want to crawl inside the tomb itself.

You might recall that, when Mary Magdalene and "the other Mary" visited Jesus' tomb on Easter morning, they found the huge stone had been rolled away (Mark 16:4). (The stone at the door of this particular New Testament tomb is very small. Some huge tombs have been found, sealed with very large stones, as described in Mark.)

When you have returned to the courtyard in front of the church, you may want to refresh yourself. The bathroom is off to the LEFT, and you can also refill your canteens with fresh water.

Once outside the gate turn RIGHT (bearing left) and up the hill. We are heading for the Mount of Olives, about a fifteen- to twenty-minute walk. You are now walking in the very footsteps of Jesus and his disciples. For two thousand years Christian pilgrims have reenacted the Triumphal Entry by following this path.

As you walk through the Arab village of A-Tor, look about you and note the many interesting aspects of village life.

When you reach the high stone wall ahead, bear to your RIGHT and continue up the hill. A few minutes more, and you are at the top of the Mount of Olives. At the top of the hill, stop and look out to your LEFT.

## MOUNT OF OLIVES

The area that appears to be shimmering way out in the distance is the Dead Sea, the lowest point on the land surface of the earth, 1,296 feet below the level of the Mediterranean. This is the desert from which Jesus came up to Jerusalem. It is also the area where John the Baptist carried out his work.

Continue along the same path you have been walking on, and you will shortly arrive at the main street of the Mount of Olives. When you reach it, turn LEFT. You can get something to refresh yourself at any of the several quick snack shops here. Or cross the street and rest awhile in the park.

## Jesus' Ascension

We are going to visit two sites of the Ascension now. To be chronologically exact, we should view them on the last day, but that would entail a return visit to this area. So, to be practical, we will visit them now while we are here on the Mount of Olives.

Turning LEFT as you enter the road, walk a minute or so until you reach the building set back a bit from the road. There is a minaret on the right side of the building, and our great friend the camel master is usually on duty in front.

## Mohammed, the Camel Master

The lovely gentleman next to his camel is our dear friend Mohammed. On Friday mornings, when Mohammed is at prayer in the mosque, his son Jacob is on duty.

SHU-SHU THE KISSING CAMEL

Shu-Shu, his camel, is seventeen years old (as of this writing) and has a life expectancy of thirty-five years. He eats thirty pounds of oats and two stacks of hay daily but drinks only once a week—twenty-eight gallons at a time. And, yes, Shu-Shu will "kiss" visitors. Ask Mohammed to take a picture of you being kissed by Shu-Shu.

Behind Shu-Shu and Mohammed is the entrance to a mosque that commemorates the Ascension of Jesus. Sorry, visitors are not allowed inside. Enter the courtyard through the gray metal doors ahead. The masque and the Church of the Holy Ascension are near each other, but are separate.

**CHURCH OF THE HOLY ASCENSION**

## Church of the Holy Ascension

The Church of the Ascension is open daily, including Sunday, 8 A.M. to 6 P.M. The site, also known as the Inbomon ("High Place"), is shared by both Christians and Muslims, since Jesus is acknowledged in the Koran as a Prophet of God. This building was originally constructed by the Byzantines in A.D. 378, who left the chapel in the center open to the sky as a symbol of the Ascension. It was enclosed by a dome by Saladin in A.D. 1187 when he converted it to a mosque; was then reconverted as a church.

Inside we see a rock (enclosed by a frame) that has a footlike impression on its face. Local tradition has inspired stories about this "footprint," which is the reason this area is considered a place of the Ascension. The depression in the rock was thought to be Jesus' footprint as he ascended.

Behind the rock is a niche in the wall. This is a Muslim prayer niche, facing the most holy of Islamic cities, Mecca. It is called a *mihrab*. Koran, Sura (Chapter) IV: 158 CF-111-55: "God raised Him [Jesus] up unto Himself." Candles are available in the niche.

As you exit into the courtyard, bear LEFT and start to walk around the building. Pay special attention to the capitals of the gray-stone columns around the outside of the building. These are Crusader capitals. Notice that some have strange birds carved into the stone.

On the outer walls of the building, running all around the courtyard walls, are hooks and rings. These are provided to accommodate the tents of the pilgrims who visit this site to celebrate the feast of the Ascension. Acts 1: 9–11:

> And when he [Jesus] had spoken these things, while they beheld, he was taken up: and a cloud received him out of their sight.
>
> And while they looked stedfastly toward heaven, as he went up, behold, two men stood by them in white apparel,
>
> Which also said, Ye men of Galilee, why stand ye gazing up into heaven? This same Jesus, which is taken up from you into heaven, shall so come in like manner as ye have seen him go into heaven.

The feast of the Ascension occurs exactly forty days after Easter. A twenty-four hour prayer service is held there. Five Christian churches pitch tents the night before and hold services in this courtyard: the Armenians, the Copts, the Syrians, the Greek Orthodox, and the Roman Catholics. To maintain a sense of orderliness within the compound, each group is assigned a specific altar area to conduct its own services. They use the base of the columns along the walls plus portable altars.

Leave through the same doors by which you entered. Turn LEFT on the road in front and walk ahead a very short distance to the last stop on this walk:

## The Church of the Pater Noster (The Church of the Lord's Prayer)

The Church of the Pater Noster is open daily 8:30 to 11:45 A.M. and 3 to 4:30 P.M. Built by Crusaders and maintained today by the French government, this church is dedicated to the Lord's Prayer. *Pater Noster* is Latin for "Our Father," the opening words.

We will be visiting the following sites in here:

- Grotto of the Lord's Prayer
- Tomb of the Princess
- Grotto of the Eleona Church
- Crypt of the Credo

Walk inside and turn LEFT to

## The Grotto of the Lord's Prayer

As you approach the entrance, look on the LEFT wall at the silver chromium plaque. It is the Lord's Prayer in Braille. We are going to see the Lord's Prayer in sixty languages. This is dedicated to the memory of Jesus teaching his disciples how to pray. Matthew 6:9–13:

> After this manner therefore pray ye: Our Father, which art in Heaven, Hallowed be Thy name.
>
> Thy kingdom come, Thy will be done in earth, as it is in heaven.
>
> Give us this day our daily bread: And forgive us our debts, as we forgive our debtors.

And lead us not into temptation but deliver us from evil: For thine is the kingdom and the power and the glory, forever. Amen.

Walk straight ahead. You will pass a brown door, which is the entrance to the convent of the Carmelite Sisters. This order of nuns have dedicated their lives to seclusion and prayer. Please do not try to enter.

Turn RIGHT past the door. You will find yourself in a very beautiful Crusader room with a classic Gothic ceiling, an excellent setting for a photograph. Up ahead is a memorial to the very remarkable woman who is directly responsible for the Pater Noster complex.

## The Princess

Her name was Princess de la Tour d'Auvergne. She was a woman who loved the Lord's Prayer very deeply. She arrived in Jerusalem in 1856 and lived here for eight years. She commissioned the chancellor of the French consulate in Jerusalem to search for the ruins of the Byzantine church that was built by Constantine on this same site. Charles Clermont-Ganneau, a celebrated French archaeologist, whom she hired, did indeed come upon the remains of the Eleona Church, from the Byzantine times. You are looking at

## The Tomb of the Princess

She left Jerusalem and returned to her home in Florence, Italy, and died there at the age of eighty. Her last wish was that she be buried in the Pater Noster, which had been so much a part of her life. She actually posed for the marble statue in front of you. She had the ashes of her father's heart brought here and placed in a bronze urn. You can see it on the sill of the window above the crypt.

A RIGHT turn brings us to the lovely grotto.

We think it's important to learn a little about the history of the original Byzantine church on this site. It was called

## The Eleona Church

The remains of this, the original church, are all underground and not visible to us today. It was built at the behest of Helena, mother of the Emperor Constantine, and named for the surrounding olive groves (*elaion* in Greek). The Persians destroyed the building in 614, and the Crusaders rebuilt, naming it the Pater Noster ("Our Father") Church. And, as we have seen, its ruins were rescued by the princess in the 1850s. Thus it has a thoroughly royal heritage.

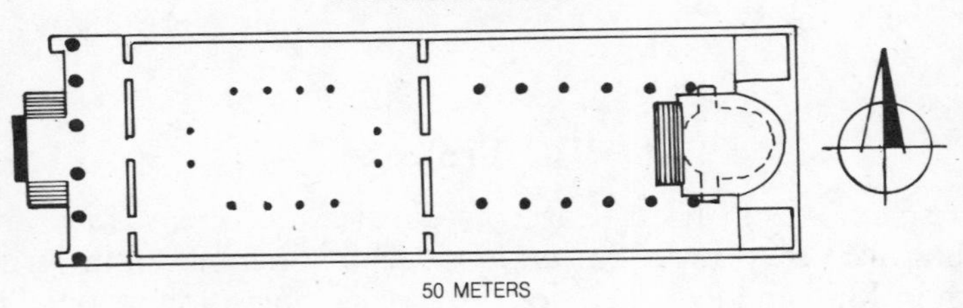


ELEONA CHURCH FLOOR PLAN

Helena came to the Holy Land in her old age, seeking the sites of major events in Jesus' life. Her son built three major churches at her suggestion in and around Jerusalem.

CHURCHES BUILT BY CONSTANTINE:

| EVENT | CHURCH |
|---|---|
| Jesus' Birth | Church of the Nativity, Bethlehem |
| Jesus' Death | Church of the Holy Sepulcher |
| Jesus' Teachings | The Eleona Church |

An early written source places a Constantine church on the Mount of Olives. Eusebius (265–340) in his *History of the Church* (324) writes:

> The mother of the Emperor raised a stately structure on the Mount of Olives, also in memory of His Ascent to Heaven who is the Saviour of mankind, erecting a sacred church and temple on the very summit of the Mount of Olives.

The New Testament tells us that prior to his Ascension, Jesus held meetings with his disciples. Then, when he completed his teachings, he went to another high place and ascended to Heaven. His disciples asked him many questions regarding the End of Days. Matthew 24:3:

> And as he sat upon the Mount of Olives, his disciples came unto him privately, saying, Tell us, when shall these things be? and what shall be the sign of thy coming, and the end of the world?

We suggest that you find a quiet place in the grotto of this church, take out your Bible, and turn to Matthew, Chapters 24 and 25. When you have finished your readings, turn and go down the stairs to the RIGHT of the exit and head toward the entrance to the cave a few feet down the path. You are entering

## The Crypt of the Credo

On the LEFT beyond the movable barrier (you can go down if you like for a look) are ancient burial tombs from the New Testament times. Here are two things to note:

**Inscription on Mosaic Floor.** Find the inscription. It appears to the untrained eye to be the Lord's Prayer written in Hebrew; actually it is written in another language called Aramaic. This was the language of Jesus' time; it is believed to be the language that Jesus spoke and wrote.

**Ancient Graffiti.** Examine the low circular wall carefully. Notice the sign of the cross, which has been incised into several stones by visiting pilgrims. This was a normal custom, practiced for hundreds of years. We will see more examples of this graffitti when we visit the Holy Sepulcher Church on the last walk.

Now please leave by the opening opposite the one by which you entered. Walking around to the LEFT, you will see the beginnings of a very large and impressive church. Notice up front the stone chair and benches. This design was copied from the original Eleona Church. They had to stop construction at the outbreak of World War I when the funding ran out; it was later decided to leave it as you see it today, unfinished.

Retrace your steps to the exit of this church complex. When you again reach the Mount of Olives road, turn LEFT and begin walking down the hill. Cross to the other side of the road. You will be walking along a low stone wall. Stop anywhere along here, to enjoy, just as Jesus and his disciples did, a good close-up view of Jerusalem and the Holy Temple. To help you identify various sites, turn to Orientation Guide, page 76.

What you are looking at below, where the golden and slate gray domes are, is the Temple Mount. In Jesus' day, it would have been surmounted by the great Temple itself, which dominated not only the Mount but the entire city:

MODEL OF THE SECOND TEMPLE, AS IT LOOKED IN JESUS' DAY

Even if you would like to continue with the next walk, you can't. Most of the churches on the Mount of Olives are closed for a couple of hours every afternoon. We suggest that you do one of two things:

1. Take a lunch break till 3 P.M. and then continue with Walk 2.
2. Call it a day and start Walk 2 tomorrow morning at 8 A.M.

## GETTING BACK TO THE CITY

**By Bus to East Jerusalem.** Walk ahead and to your left, and you will be able to take the No. 75 bus, which stops at the Central Bus Station across from the Damascus Gate in East Jerusalem.

**By Bus to West Jerusalem.** As above take the No. 75 bus to the Central Bus Station in East Jerusalem. There change for a city Egged bus, either the No. 23 or No. 27, and in a short time you will be in West Jerusalem.

**By Taxi.** Walk ahead and to the left, up the incline, and you will be at a taxi stand in front of the Intercontinental Hotel.

We hope you enjoyed today's first tour, and that it was a learning experience for you.

## ROUTE OF WALK 2

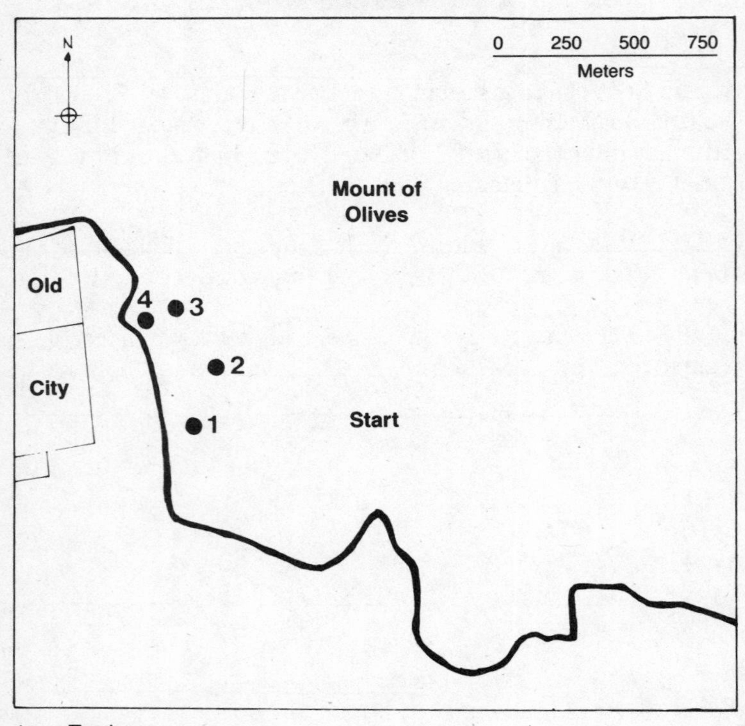


1 Tombs
2 Dominus Flvit
3 Russian Church
4 Garden of Gethsemane

WALK

# 2

## *The Mount of Olives*

| SITE | EVENT |
|---|---|
| • Top of the Mount of Olives | Overview: Mountain in Jesus' Day |
| • Tombs of Haggai and Malachi | |
| • Church of Dominus Flevit | Jesus weeps for Jerusalem |
| • The Golden Gate | Messianic expectations |
| • Garden of Gethsemane | Prayer, betrayal, arrest |
| • Church of All Nations | Agony in the Garden |

Today's tour goal is to re-create the physical, political, and religious facets of life during Jesus' time, and to relive his last night on earth, when he went to pray with his disciples in the Garden of Gethsemane and was betrayed there by Judas.

### GETTING TO THE STARTING POINT

The starting point for today's walk is the platform below the Intercontinental Hotel.

**By Bus from West Jerusalem.** There is no direct bus from West Jerusalem. Take bus No. 23 or 27 from the Central Bus Station on Jaffa Road and get off near the Damascus Gate in East

Jerusalem. Across the street you will find the Central Bus Station in East Jerusalem. Below are the instructions from there.

**By Bus from East Jerusalem.** Go to the Central Bus Station opposite the Damascus Gate and take the Egged bus No. 42. Check the time of the next bus, as it only runs three times a day. This will take you to the door of the Intercontinental Hotel. The Arab bus No. 75 runs more frequently, and it also goes to our starting point. Don't be concerned when you see the bus make a left turn when you reach the top of the hill. It will make a U turn and come back to the hotel.

**By Car.** Head toward the Damascus Gate in East Jerusalem. Go past the gate and keep going straight until you reach the end of the road. When you get to the end of the road, make a wide LEFT, and follow the road, bearing to your RIGHT. When you reach the very top of the steep hill, turn RIGHT, and in three minutes you will be at the starting point in front of the Intercontinental Hotel.

## THE MOOD OF THE PEOPLE

The Jews of Jerusalem were an occupied people. Their civil liberties were dictated by Rome, as well as their civil laws. Roman soldiers occupied the city in vast numbers. The relationship between the Roman soldiers and the citizens of Jerusalem was very strained.

The Romans wisely left the administration of the Temple to the Jewish high priest. However, the high priesthood was a political appointment, its occupant chosen by Romans and loyal to them. Most Jews found not being able to practice their religion without Roman interference more abusive than all the other restrictions imposed on them by Rome.

### The City Prepares for a Festival

Along with Jesus and His disciples, thousands upon thousands of other pilgrims came to Jerusalem to celebrate the holiday of Passover and to offer their sacrifices at the Temple.

As mentioned above, the seeds for a revolt against Rome had already been planted and were growing. It is interesting to note that the masses who welcomed Jesus did so by waving palm branches. The Palm Branch was used as a symbol of Jewish Independence by the Hasmonaeans (Maccabees) when they won their independence from the Greeks about a hundred years earlier. The first coins they minted after the victory show a stylized palm tree:

MACCABEE COINS

## Messianic Expectations

Even though Jesus saw himself as a religious reformer, the crowds greeting him on his Triumphal Entry may have been waving the palm branches as a show of political support for independence. But in addition to seeking a charismatic political leader, the people were also in need of religious leadership with which they could identify. With the raising of Lazarus, Jesus aroused these feelings and hopes in the people of Jerusalem.

They greeted him and the disciples with shouts of Hosanna (God Save Us). By entering the city on a donkey, Jesus fulfilled the biblical prophesy. Zachariah 9:9 and Matthew 21:9:

> Rejoice greatly, O daughter of Zion; shout O daughter of Jerusalem; behold, thy King cometh unto thee; he is just, and having salvation; lowly, and riding upon an ass, and upon a colt, the foal of an ass.
>
> And the multitudes that went before, and that followed, cried, saying, Hosanna to the Son of David: Blessed is he that cometh in the name of the Lord! Hosanna in the highest.

## MOUNT OF OLIVES

What would Jesus have seen standing where you are, 2,680 feet above sea level, and looking down into the city? In order to re-create this mountain as it may have appeared two thousand years ago, we ask you to use your imagination.

Walk to the end of the platform below the Intercontinental Hotel and look out. Imagine every building you see in front of you taken away. In their place stand thousands of olive trees. In your mind's eye, color the leaves silvery white since that is how they look in spring, the time of the year that Jesus spent his last week in Jerusalem.

### The Kidron Valley

Look all the way down to the bottom of the mountain. If we could remove about fifty feet of dirt, we would then reach the ground level of the Kidron Valley in Jesus' time. That's how much soil has built up over the last two thousand years. Every rainfall and windstorm adds to the accumulation.

### The Eastern Wall

Looking at the Old City, concentrate on the wall running around it. That's the Eastern Wall. This is the only wall of the Temple Mount that was not altered by King Herod the Great when he enlarged the Mount in order to build what is commonly known as the Second Temple. The significance of this is that there is a very good chance that the foundation stones of this wall existed in Jesus' day. Even though the wall you see today was built by Turkish Sultan Suleiman the Magnificent (1496–1566), the original wall must certainly have appeared the same to Jesus.

### The Golden Gate

Sometimes it's a bit difficult to spot the Golden Gate in the Eastern Wall. The picture (opposite) should help you locate it.

GOLDEN GATE

Follow the line of the wall going to the RIGHT. The Golden Gate is the raised portion with the double arches, which are blocked in. It has long been associated with the Coming of the Messiah.

## The Second Temple

Look at the Golden Dome up on the Mount. This is a Muslim shrine called the Dome of the Rock. In Jesus' time, it did not yet exist. In its place put the Second Temple of King Herod the Great, in all of its magnificence and splendor. It completely dominated not only the city of Jerusalem but in a spiritual sense many other parts of the world.

Although there are no remains of it today, it is where Jesus prayed and taught the people when he was in Jerusalem. He also studied here as a young man. The Temple was about seventeen stories high, faced in marble and trimmed in gold. Now let's see the city as it looks today, two thousand years after Jesus.

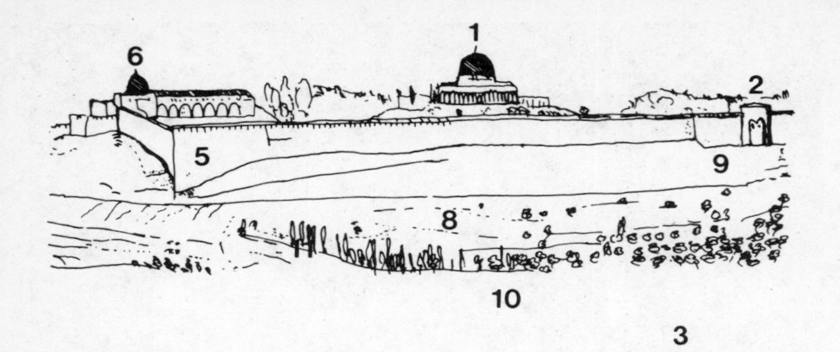


**ORIENTATION GUIDE**

1. Dome of the Rock (Temple area in Jesus' time);
2. Golden Gate;
3. Russian Church (golden onion domes);
4. Dominus Flevit Church (black/white);
5. Eastern City Wall;
6. El Aqsa Mosque (slate gray dome);
7. Jewish cemetery;
8. Christian cemetery;
9. Muslim cemetery;
10. Garden of Gethsemane.

Note: Nos. 3, 4, 7, and 10 are not visible from where you are standing; the numbers give the approximate location.

We are now standing on the ridge of the Mount of Olives. It got its name from the fact that olive trees have been growing here for at least three thousand years. It is a chalk mountain. Most other trees cannot survive in chalk, but olive trees are an exception. Turn to your RIGHT and walk along until you reach the orange sign that says "Common Graves." Now turn LEFT down the staircase. When you reach the bottom of the steps turn LEFT. Go through the gates that have the blue sign on top, which indicates that these are the

**MODEL OF THE SECOND TEMPLE, BUILT BY KING HEROD THE GREAT**

## TOMBS OF THE PROPHETS HAGGAI AND MALACHI

One of two brothers will greet you with a warm welcome and a friendly smile. Harbi Ottman and his brother Jamin have taken over from their father and are the official caretakers of this site. They live with their families right here on top of the Tombs. If you are lucky, they might invite you for a cup of tea, and if so, please don't refuse. This is an Arab's way of showing hospitality. They will give you a wonderful tour of the Tombs in English. It is customary to offer them a small gratuity for this service.

Haggai and Malachi were Old Testament prophets. Haggai lived in the sixth century B.C., during the period of the return of the Jews from the Babylonian Captivity. Malachi was born about a century later. Jewish tradition places their tombs here along with that of Zechariah (eighth century B.C.). Later, during the fourth or fifth centuries, Christian pilgrims who died during their trip were likewise buried here. We will point out one niche with a cross incised over it. Let's now go down into the Tombs below. They are open daily, 8 A.M. to 5 P.M.

Please walk carefully. The steps are worn and steep. Once inside LOOK UP. That large hole tells us how these Tombs were dug. The underground cave into which the tombs were cut is six feet deep and four feet long. During the Jordanian occupation of East Jerusalem from 1948 to 1967, they desecrated these tombs by using them as garbage dumps. The basic layout of this site is two half-circular tunnels. The outer tunnel contains fifty tombs, the inner one none. Walk toward either wall in front of you. Notice the niches cut into the rock. These are washing basins.

Jewish custom requires all who visit a grave to wash their hands upon leaving. They provided for this by cutting two basins for water into the wall at the exit of the Tombs. Put your hand in and touch the original clay pipes they used for the runoff. Please don't take a souvenir. Now let's walk through the outer tunnel. Turn RIGHT, and as you enter the tunnel, count the holes in the rocks (catacombs), and stop in front of the seventh one. Shine your light on the cross above the catacomb. Harbi or Jamin will point out the children's tombs as well as the traditional tombs of the prophets Haggai and Malachi and a suspected tomb of Zechariah.

When you have finished your tour of this site, leave by the same staircase you first entered. We hope you enjoyed this visit. Even though it is not a New Testament site, we felt that since you were here already, you might enjoy seeing it. As you leave the property, turn LEFT down the hill. In a minute or two you will reach the entrance to a church whose gray metal doors will be on the RIGHT. This is

## THE CHURCH OF DOMINUS FLEVIT ("THE LORD WEPT")

This church is located on the traditional site of Jesus' weeping over the coming destruction of Jerusalem. Walk in and take the path straight ahead. Those low buildings you are passing off to the RIGHT probably interest you. Don't worry; we are going to return to them and study the archaeological finds that were made at this site.

Just follow the path, and it will lead you to the entrance of the church. The first church on this site was built by the Byzantines in the fifth century. Today's Franciscan church was designed by Italian architect A. Barluzzi and erected in 1955. The visiting hours are 8 to 11:30 A.M., 3 to 5 P.M., including Sunday.

**THE TEAR-SHAPED DOME OF DOMINUS FLEVIT**

However, before you reach the church entrance, stop anywhere along the path and study the black and white building in front of you.

## A Tear Drop

Since the site is dedicated to the memory of Jesus' weeping, the architect designed the building in the shape of a tear drop, with four vials for catching the running tears on each corner of the roof.

Before going inside the church, let's examine the ancient mosaic floor to the LEFT of the entrance.

## A Byzantine Floor

This floor is from the first (Byzantine) church built on this site to commemorate Jesus weeping over the coming destruction of the city. It was destroyed in the Persian invasion in 614. Notice the representations of fish, grain, grapes, etc.

ANCIENT MOSAIC FLOOR

## The Apse

Like the mosaic the apse is part of the original church built on this site about fifteen hundred years ago. Notice that the altar of this original church is directed to the east. This is normal in every major Catholic and Eastern Orthodox church. The reason we make mention of this is that, when we enter the modern church of Dominus Flevit, we find the altar facing the opposite way, west. We will explain why inside.

Enter the church. If a service is in session, please be patient; take a seat and wait until they finish the service before you begin moving around. As you enter, notice the Franciscan cross carved into the wooden doors. Once inside, take a seat and get comfortable.

## The Altar

As we mentioned outside, it faces west. The architect, A. Barluzzi, wanted to emphasize Jesus' looking out over the city as he predicted its destruction. The destruction is the theme of this church. Luke 19:41:

> And when he was come near, he beheld the city and wept over it.

**Symbols.** In the center, a Ciborium (vessel for holding the Host); below it, the Crown of Thorns. Now turn your attention to the mosaic on the altar.

This mosaic depicts a mother hen protecting her brood of chicks, symbolizing Jesus' love for his city. Matthew 23:37:

> O Jerusalem, Jerusalem . . . how often would I have gathered thy children together, even as a hen gathereth her chickens under her wing, and ye would not!

THE WINDOW WITH GRILLE

ALTAR MOSAIC

Here is a shortened version of the predicted destruction, for those who are not carrying their Bibles today. Matthew 24:2 and 16–21:

> And Jesus said unto them, See ye not all these things? Verily I say unto you, There shall not be left here one stone upon another, that shall not be thrown down.
>
> Then let them which be in Judaea flee into the mountains:
>
> Let him which is on the housetop not come down to take anything out of his house:
>
> Neither let him which is in the field return back to take his clothes.
>
> And woe unto them that are with child, and to them that give suck in those days!
>
> But pray your flight be not in the winter, neither on the sabbath day:
>
> For then shall be great tribulation, such as was not since the beginning of the world to this time, no, nor ever shall be.

Now please look up at the frescoes on the wall, using the one above the altar as a starting point.

## Wall Frescoes/Reliefs

**Above altar.** The Triumphal Entry.

**Left wall.** Mary, Martha, and the mother of Jesus, Mary.

**Right wall.** Disciples overlooking the city.

**Rear wall.** Destruction of Jerusalem by the Romans in A.D. 70.

Also notice the plaques representing the fourteen Stations of the Cross along the walls.

Lastly, note the inscription on the left wall, which is the wall opposite the door. It is the Latin for Luke 19:41–44:

> And when he was come near, he beheld the city, and wept over it.
>
> Saying, If thou hadst known, even thou, at least in this thy day, the things which belong unto thy peace! but now they are hid from thine eyes.

> For the days shall come upon thee, that thine enemies shall cast a trench about thee, and compass thee round, and keep thee in on every side.
>
> And shall lay thee even with the ground, and thy children within thee; and they shall not leave in thee one stone upon another; because thou knewest not the time of thy visitation.

As you exit from the church follow the path to the low stone wall overlooking the Old City in the distance. Look out over the wall at the

## Tombstones (The Necropolis)

Interestingly enough, the Mount of Olives could as well have been named the Mount of Cemeteries. It has been used for burials for over three thousand years and is the oldest known Jewish cemetery in the world. Not only Jews are buried in this area, for the Christian cemetery is in the bottom of the Kidron Valley, just below, and the Muslim one along the Eastern Wall. Considering that the Kidron is also called the Valley of

TOMBS ON THE MOUNT OF OLIVE

Jehosaphat, this could be seen as a fulfillment of the prophecy of Joel. Joel 3:2:

> I will also gather all nations and will bring them down into the Valley of Jehosaphat.

Generations have believed that when the Messiah returns, he will come from the east and enter the Temple. Those who are buried here will be the first to enter heaven on that judgment day.

Now look at the Golden Gate, which we spotted at the beginning of our walk.

## The Golden Gate

The gate was sealed in A.D. 638, during the first Arab period, probably for religious reasons. It is of course located above the Valley of Judgment. For when the Messiah comes, he will enter the city through the Golden Gate.

GOLDEN GATE

Is this the original Golden Gate? The evidence says no. Today's gate was built in the sixth or seventh century A.D. In 1969 a dear friend of mine, Yaacov (Jim) Fleming, director of the Jerusalem Center for Biblical Studies, made an accidental discovery of a double arch below the Golden Gate of today. Yaacov was doing fieldwork just after a torrential rain, and the ground in front of the gate gave way under him. He found himself in a mass burial grave among human bones, and with his camera he took a photograph of a double arch directly under the present Golden Gate. By the time he had returned with the Israeli archaeologists, Muslim authorities had already filled in the grave and cemented it over.

GOLDEN DOMES OF THE RUSSIAN CHURCH

You might be wondering why Israel has not continued to excavate at this most important historical site. The answer is that all sites on the Temple Mount and especially the Muslim cemetery along the Eastern Wall were put under the control of the Muslim council by the Israeli government after the Six Day War. It is the official government policy of the state of Israel that all Christian and Muslim holy sites be controlled by their respective religions. So this gate below might have been the original gate. Only further scientific research can let us know for sure.

Before leaving here, please notice the beautiful golden onion domes of the Russian Church of Saint Mary Magdalene. It is considered by many to be among the most striking architecture in Jerusalem. Certainly worth a picture or two.

Now you are in for an

## Archaeological Treat

To get to the next stop here at Dominus Flevit, walk to the LEFT and follow the same path you entered. Go up the seven steps on the left, and walk until you reach very tall trees. Turn LEFT in here and head for the stone building ahead. In the church are lime-

TWO SARCOPHAGI—BURIALS FROM JESUS' TIME

stone coffins called sarcophagi, a common form of burial in Jesus' day. The word "sarcophagi" is Greek and literally translated means "flesh eaters." The coffin is limestone, a porous rock, and as the dampness seeps into the coffin, it speeds up the decomposition of the corpse.

Notice the differences between the two. The box on the LEFT has a very smooth finish. The one on the RIGHT has a rough finish. This is evidence that the smooth one is carved from chalk, which is a very soft material, while in contrast the other one is from hard limestone, which is more difficult to carve.

Now notice the stone in the rear with the cross incised on it. Next to that is a storage area for some ossuaries. We will learn about ossuaries at the next stop. On your LEFT outside the building is an ossuary. Rap on it with your knuckles. Listen to the hollow ring. That tells us that it is crafted from hard limestone.

Go back down to the same path you just came up and take a LEFT. Stop at the building with three arches.

## Ossuaries(Used for Secondary Burials in Jesus' Time)

Prominent families of two thousand years ago had to prepare their tombs well in advance of a death. Jewish law required (and still does today) that a person must be buried before sundown of the day of his death. Tombs were very expensive. In order to maximize their use, the following practice came into being. About a year after the death, when the flesh had decomposed, the bones would be gathered up and placed in a special box.

The length of the box was determined by the length of the thigh bone, the longest bone in the human body. The boxes were called ossuaries. The word "ossuary" in Latin means "pertaining to bone." Like sarcophagi, ossuaries are carved out of limestone, which permits water to seep in and soften the bones.

Several of the ossuaries—those with yellowish and rust-colored fronts—were painted. The color is all that is left of the original paint of two thousand years ago. The restored arch in the rear is from the Crusader church, which once stood on this site.

**OSSUARIES SHOWING ROSETTE DESIGN**

Most ossuaries from Second Temple times were decorated with a rosette design. The petals are always grouped in numbers of three, six, nine, or twelve.

As you continue to the exit of the property, you may want to stop at the last building, which has some remains similar to those that you just saw. Once back on the road turn RIGHT and continue DOWN the hill. Take your time and walk slowly, since it is a very steep descent. As you are walking along, remember that Jesus and his disciples descended this same mountain on their way to the Temple.

Near the bottom of the hill you will see the tall entrance gates to the Russian Church. It is not a New Testament site, but if you are lucky enough to be here on a Tuesday or Thursday—9 A.M. to noon, 2 to 4 P.M., the only time this church is open for visitors—it will well repay a side trip.

## RUSSIAN CHURCH OF SAINT MARY MAGDALENE

We saw these beautiful golden domes from Dominus Flevit. As you enter the church and pay the small entrance fee, they will request that all women cover their arms and will provide you with a shawl free of charge. Take the stairs on your RIGHT, and you will be passing small houses where the nuns who care for this property live. Smell the lovely pine trees. As you reach the last staircase, stop. You now have an excellent close-up and unusual view of the Golden Gate and the Dome of the Rock, which seems to be peeping over the Old City wall. When you reach the top of the stairs, you might like to sit on the bench and take a short rest.

Take a few minutes to study the architecture of this Russian Church. It was named after the patron saint of Czar Alexander III's mother, thus the name Mary Magdalene. The actual entrance to the church is one short flight up. As you enter, one of the nuns will offer you a card: Take it. It identifies most of the paintings in this church. The cards are in several languages, English among them. When you are ready to leave, return the same way you entered. Don't forget to return the shawl you borrowed.

As you exit, locate the broken pillar set in the wall on the opposite side of the road. The wall has a green fence atop it. This shaft is

### The Traditional Pillar of Judas

This column of rose-hued stone serves as a place to remember Judas. The Latins called it *Osculum* ("Kiss") taken from Luke 22:48. It became known as the Pillar of Judas. Pilgrims as late as the twentieth century have prayed beside it.

As with the Pillar of Judas, the natural rock that you see looking inside the fence likewise has a long tradition.

### Traditional Rock of the Apostles

This is a place to remember the Apostles who accompanied Jesus to the Garden of Gethsemane, where he went to pray. Con-

THE OSCULUM

tinuing along down the hill, on your way to the Garden of Gethsemane and the Church of All Nations, notice the cross incised into the stone below the fifth green gate atop the walls. At the bottom of the hill, turn LEFT, and a few feet down on the LEFT is the entrance to

## THE GARDEN OF GETHSEMANE AND THE CHURCH OF ALL NATIONS

The Garden is open all year from 8 to 11:45 A.M.; the afternoon hours are 2:30 to 6 P.M. from April to September, and 2:30 to 5 P.M. from October to March. We suggest that you go inside the Garden and read the story of the New Testament that took place in this area. Matthew 26:36–45; Mark 14:32–41.

A SINGLE GREAT OLIVE TREE

## The Massive Olive Trees

Looking into the garden, we see beautiful old olive trees. Though they look like separate trees that have grown together, actually the opposite is true. It is one tree. The center of an olive tree rots away as it ages. So in effect it is one tree you are looking at. These trees are dated to about fifteen hundred years ago, according to the Volcani Institute in Israel. This is important for us since it tells us they were planted about five hundred years after Jesus.

What happened to the olive trees of Jesus' time? In the year A.D. 70, about forty years or so after Jesus' death, the Romans totally destroyed Jerusalem.

The Herodian stones with which the city was built are limestone. When they are heated to a high temperature, steam is created, and this causes the limestone to burst open. The Romans, in preparing to burn the city, cut down all the trees for a twelve-mile radius around Jerusalem. They then used the wood to build fires against the wall. Once the stones were loosened, they simply pushed them over with iron rods.

Olive trees have been used to express many analogies in the New Testament. An example is in the Epistle of Paul when he reminds Christians of their Jewish roots. Romans 11:1 and 16:

> I say then, Hath God cast away his people? God forbid. For I also am an Israelite, of the seed of Abraham, of the tribe of Benjamin. . . .
>
> For if the firstfruit be holy, the lump is also holy. And if the root be holy, so are the branches.

Tradition has it that this is where Jesus began his Passion, suffered, was betrayed, and arrested. Jesus and his disciples, having finished the Last Supper up on Mount Zion, returned to the Garden of Gethsemane to pray during the night. Matthew 26:26:

> Then cometh Jesus with them unto a place called Gethsemane and saith unto his disciples, Sit ye here, while I go and pray yonder.

Jesus told three of his disciples to walk a little distance away from the others and to accompany him. He then went a short distance away from the three to pray, and in his agony he sweat blood. But when he returned to them, he found that they had all fallen asleep. Matthew 26:41:

> Watch and pray [Jesus rebuked them] that ye enter not into temptation; the spirit indeed is willing, but the flesh is weak.

Judas approached with the armed guards. He had told them that he would identify Jesus by greeting him with a kiss. Luke 22:47–48:

> And while he yet spake, behold a multitude, and he that was called Judas, one of the twelve, went before them, and drew near unto Jesus, to kiss him.
>
> But Jesus said unto him, Judas, betrayest thou the Son of man with a kiss?

As the soldiers reached for Jesus, Peter drew his sword and cut off the ear of one of them named Malchus. Jesus admonished Peter. Matthew 26:52:

> All they that take the sword, shall perish with the sword.

FLASHLIGHT ON.

Now it is time to go inside the church. It is very beautiful, but very dark inside. So before going in, first read about what you are going to look for inside.

## THE CHURCH OF ALL NATIONS (OR THE BASILICA OF THE AGONY)

The first church on this site, built by the Byzantines in the fourth century, was destroyed by the Persians in 614. The second church

**MAIN ENTRANCE TO CHURCH OF ALL NATIONS**

was erected by the Crusaders, and this third building, designed by Barluzzi (who also designed Dominus Flevit), was erected in 1924.

The theme of this church is a garden at nighttime on a chilly spring evening. Inside the building, look for the following:

**The Ceiling.** The sky with reflecting stars.

**The Columns.** Olive trees whose slivers of branches are visible where they meet the dome of the ceiling.

CEILING SHOWING MEDALLION AND STARS

**The Windows.** The Passion. The windows are made in alabaster stone, which is translucent rather than transparent. The violet light shining through reflects the liturgical purple, associated both with mourning and with royalty.

**The Bedrock.** This outcrop is reputed to be the spot where Jesus prayed and suffered the Bloody Sweat, or the Agony in the Garden. To the faithful it represents submission to the will of God.

ALABASTER
WINDOW

OCTCROP WITH
THORNY GRILLE

**Grille Surrounding the Rock.** This interwoven, thorny grille represents the tangle of the political and social climate that Jesus was caught up in and which eventually overtook him.

**Silver Doves on the Grille.** They symbolize Jesus' innocence: caught in the brambles of the fence, their necks extended like meek sacrificial victims, in that very last moment before death.

**The Altar.** The stone below the altar has been cut in the shape of a wine cup. "Let this cup pass from me." The stone was especially chosen for the red veins running through it, symbolizing Jesus' sweating so profusely that he was actually shedding drops of blood, a condition called hematidrosis.

**Mosaic Above Altar.** Jesus appears strained yet calm. The hand of God bearing a wreath of eventual victory seems to assure him that he is not alone. His disciples can be seen sleeping beside the trunks of the olive trees.

**The Statues.** The evangelists are shown each holding a book and inscription.

SILVER DOVES

**The Mosaic Floor.** Walk over to the glass panel in any of the places you are near. Below the glass, under today's floor, is the original Byzantine floor from the first church built on this site. To the untrained eye the modern and ancient floors seem to have the same pattern, but they are not identical. The design runs in opposite directions from each other. Could this have been done so that when future archaeologists study the ruins of today's floor they will not confuse it with the earlier one?

Now walk to the center of the church and LOOK UP at the domes. The modern name of this church is the Church of All Nations. It got its name from the fact that many Catholic nations donated the funds to rebuild it. In the center of each dome is an insignia plaque of the nation that contributed. Before leaving, you might also note the wall mosaics. Orient yourself by facing the altar.

**Left wall.** The betrayal kiss by Judas.

**Center wall.** A depiction of the Agony in the Garden.

**Right wall.** Jesus identifies himself to the arresting officers. John 18:5:

> They answered him, Jesus of Nazareth. Jesus saith unto them, I am he. And Judas also, which betrayed him, stood with them.

Leave this church the same way you entered, and when you are out past the garden, turn LEFT, and a few feet down is the main road.

Cross the road very carefully, for traffic moves fast here. Once you are across the street, turn LEFT and head for the bench up ahead. Have a seat. You earned it today. We hope that you noticed the Christian cemetery in the valley below to your RIGHT. We mentioned this cemetery earlier when we discussed the burials in the Valley of Judgment.

From where you are now, you have an excellent view of the Church of All Nations.

**MOSAICS AND STAGS OVER ENTRANCE:**

Let's study the entrance and identify each symbol we can see. At the peak of the roof stands a cross with statues of deer on either side, a reminder of Psalm 42:1:

> As the hart panteth after the water brooks, so panteth my soul after thee, O God.

On the pediment is a large mosaic, depicting a sympathetic Jesus. We see people surrounding him, placing their trust in him while they toil and suffer.

**On his left.** Lowly unfortunates, who through their tears look to him with confidence. A mother offers her child to Jesus.

**On his right.** The wise and powerful admit their shortcomings to him.

**Above.** We see an angel receiving Jesus' heart into his hands. The inscription, in Latin, is from Hebrews 5:7:

> Who in the days of his flesh, when he had offered up his prayers and supplications, with strong crying and tears, unto him that was able to save Him from death, and was heard in that he feared.

Now cross the street and walk right up to the entrance of this church. Notice the bronze doors. The Tree of Life design springs from a cross and turns downward in four volutes, each framing one of the Evangelists.

The evangelical symbols are as follows:

**John: The Eagle;** this emphasizes Jesus' divinity and his Gospel soaring to heaven.

**Matthew: Man holding a book;** this emphasizes the kindly and human aspects of Jesus' life.

**Luke: The Ox;** the ox was a traditional sacrificial animal during Jesus' times.

**Mark: The Lion;** this represents the power of the Lord.

That's the end of today's tour. I hope it was an enjoyable learning experience for you.

I suggest that you take a break for lunch now, then take Walk 4, which is the Scale Model of Jerusalem at the Holyland Hotel.

It is the shortest of all the Walks and takes about an hour and a half.

The Model is of Jerusalem in the year A.D. 66, which means you will see the city pretty much as it appeared to Jesus. Studying the Model before you actually begin the walks in the city itself will set images and pictures in your mind of how Jesus saw it.

For directions to the model turn to page 137.

## GETTING BACK TO THE CITY

**By Bus to East Jerusalem.** Facing the main entrance to the Church of All Nations, turn LEFT. You will reach the bus stop after a few steps. Take either bus No. 43 or 44. The last stop is the Damascus Gate.

**By Bus to West Jerusalem.** Same as above. When you get to the last stop, you can take a city Egged bus to West Jerusalem.

**By Taxi.** Walk ahead to the Garden of Gethsemane. There are usually several taxis waiting.

ROUTE OF WALK 3

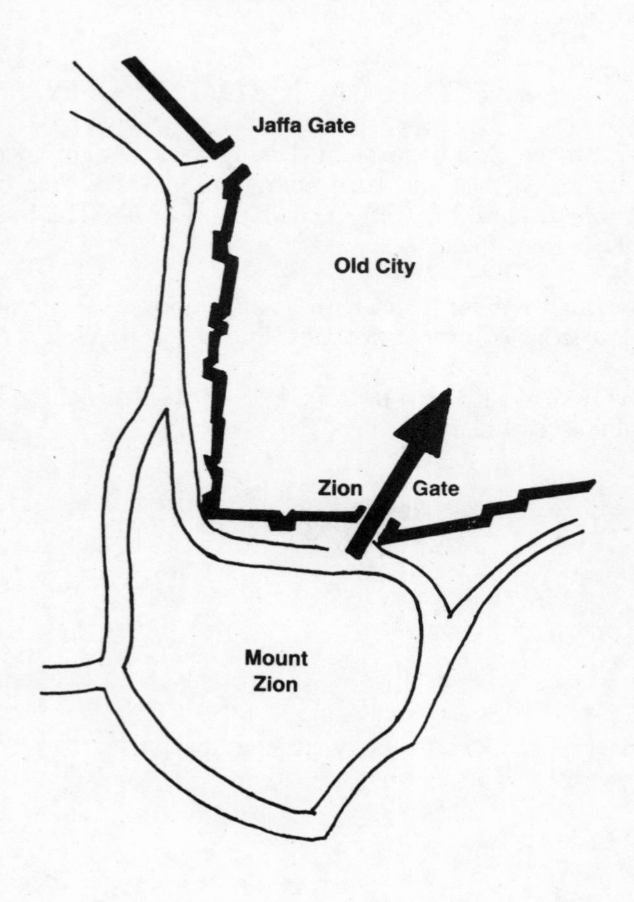

WALK

# 3

# *Mount Zion*

| EVENT | SITE |
|---|---|
| • Pentecost | Near the Dormition Church |
| • The Last Supper | The Cenacle |
| • Peter's denial and redemption | Church of Saint Peter in Gallicantu |
| • Jesus' hearing before Caiaphas | Church of Saint Peter in Gallicantu |

Today's tour goal is to visit the many New Testament sites associated with ancient Mount Zion and to relive the Last Supper, Jesus' hearing before the high priest, and Peter's subsequent denial and ultimate redemption.

## GETTING TO THE STARTING POINT

**Helpful hint if you are beginning this walk in the morning:** There is a lovely picnic area at the end of this walk, so you may want to take a picnic lunch with you today. There is a snack bar at the last stop, where you can get a soft drink or a cup of coffee. In this way you will save time if you are planning to do the walk of the Model of Jerusalem this afternoon.

The starting point for today's walk is David's Tomb on Mount Zion.

**By Bus from West Jerusalem.** Take the Egged city bus No. 1. You can pick it up at the Central Bus Station. Ask the driver to let you off at the Mount Zion stop. In Hebrew it is pronounced Har Tzion. When you descend from the bus, you will see a large green sign with white directional arrows, indicating the direction to the Western Wall, which is straight ahead, and to Mount Zion off to your LEFT. Walk back down the hill from where you got off the bus, cross the road, and take the first path to the RIGHT. Walk up this path, and in a minute or two you will see on the right the Chamber of the Holocaust. Directly opposite this complex is the entrance to David's Tomb, which is indicated by a small blue sign over the entrance gate. Enter here.

**On Foot.** Very easy! Enter the Old City through the Jaffa Gate. Bear RIGHT and take the first road to the RIGHT. Continue walking along this road for about ten minutes or so until you see a gate on the RIGHT. This is the Zion Gate. Go out this gate and turn LEFT until you reach the road. Once on the main road, turn RIGHT and walk down the hill until the first path on your RIGHT. Then follow the directions above (bus directions).

**By Car.** Drive toward the Jaffa Gate, but do not drive inside the Old City. Follow the road past the Jaffa Gate. At the very bottom of the steep hill STOP. You are going to make a LEFT turn. Please be very careful, as there is a lot of oncoming traffic at this spot. Once the road is clear, turn LEFT up the hill. In a couple of minutes you will see a sign which indicates parking, on the LEFT. Turn in here and park your car. You will see a blue sign reading "Welcome to the Diaspora Yeshiva." Take the path up the slope on the RIGHT. Then follow the directions above (bus directions).

## MOUNT ZION

Mount Zion has been revered spiritually throughout history. In poetic writings the word "Zion" is synonymous with Jerusalem. About a thousand years before Jesus, during what is referred to as the First Temple Period, Jerusalem was limited to an area called the City of David. The other name for the City of David was Zion. As the city of David expanded under King Solomon and later rulers, this hill we are now on came to be known as Mount Zion. The following New Testament quote exemplifies it best: Hebrews 12:22:

> But ye are come unto Mount Zion, and unto the city of the living God, the heavenly Jerusalem, and to an innumerable company of angels.

## Some of the Sites on Today's Walk

- An overview of Walks 1 and 2.
- The traditional Upper Room of the Last Supper.
- King David's Tomb (optional).
- An ancient stairway that Jesus may actually have walked on.
- The remains of a two-thousand-year old bakery.
- A Roman bath complex with hot and cold running water.
- A possible prison from Jesus' day.
- A maximum security cell.

I hope that program will excite you.

## SKYLINE SIGHTSEEING

Walk straight ahead into the building in front of you. You will see a large square pillar directly in front of you blocking your path. Go to the LEFT of the pillar, out the door, and walk along the arched-over walkway. You are heading for a large open courtyard with a very large pine tree. In this courtyard there is a stone staircase with a black iron railing on the RIGHT hand side. Take this staircase up four flights to the roof.

When you are standing on the roof, walk toward the domed building and looked out in the distance. We are now going to do some skyline sighting.

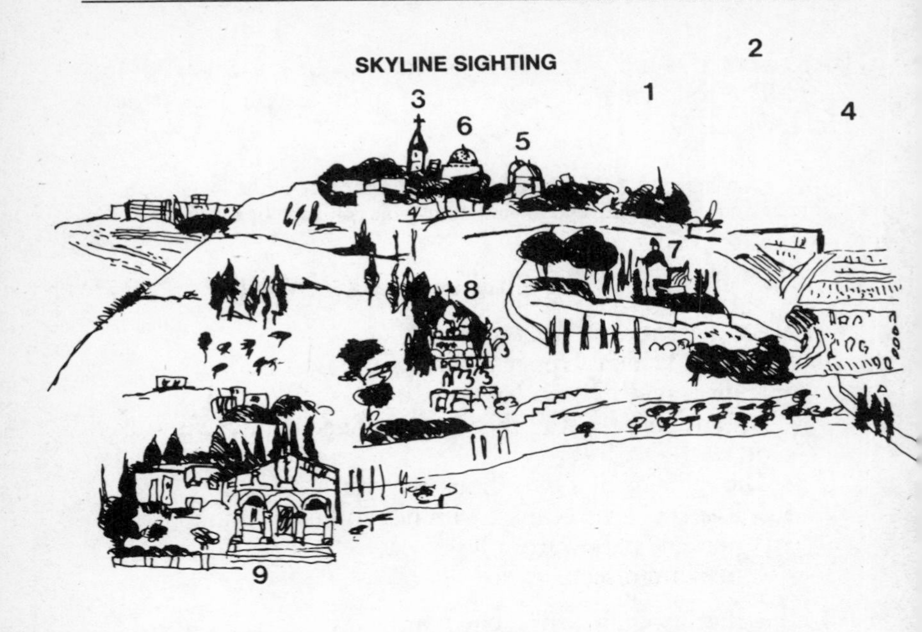


1. Judean Desert
2. Moab Mountains in Jordan
3. Tower of Ascension
4. Direction of Bethpage and Bethany
5. Church of Pater Noster
6. Church of the Ascension
7. Church of Dominus Flevit
8. Russian Church
9. Garden of Gethsemane

Note: Nos. 1, 2, and 4 are not visible from where you are standing; the numbers give the approximate locations.

Try to spot the places you visited on your first two walks. Look STRAIGHT AHEAD. Those sandy colored hills are the Judean Desert (No. 1 on the drawing). Now look way out in the distance, and if it is a clear day, you should be able to see the Moab Mountains in Jordan (No. 2 on the drawing); they will appear to have a purplish hue. The next sighting is an easy one. Locate the Tower of Ascension (No. 3); it is, of course, the Bell Tower on the ridge of the Mount of Olives in front of you. A couple of miles beyond it are Bethany and Bethpage (No. 4). Using the Tower of Ascension as a landmark look RIGHT of it and follow the

TOWER OF ASCENSION

DOMINUS FLEVIT

RUSSIAN CHURCH

line of trees. The building with the large dome on the rear of the roof and the small dome on the front of the roof is the Church of Pater Noster (No. 5).

Continue looking LEFT, and notice the mosque located right next to the Church of the Ascension (No. 6), where we met Mohammed the Camel Master and Shu-Shu. In order to spot some of these landmarks, you might have to shift positions a bit from time to time. As we travel down the Mount of Olives with our eyes, spot the Church of Dominus Flevit (No. 7); this tear-shaped building with the black roof is not difficult to find. Below this church and a little to the left is, of course, the Russian Church (No. 8) with its beautiful onion domes glistening in gold. Not visible from this roof but a bit to the RIGHT of the Russian Church and at the very bottom of the hill is of course the Garden of Gethsemane (No. 9).

## Today's Walk

Today's Walk will recall the events that took place before and after Jesus' visits to the Garden of Gethsemane—the Last Supper here on Mount Zion and, after his arrest in the Garden, the hearing before High Priest Caiaphas, which we will recount at the Church of Saint Peter in Gallicantu.

## The Domed Roofs

Notice that most homes in the Old City have domed roofs. The same was true in Jesus' time, for this type of construction has been in use for thousands of years in this part of the world. It is really very practical for several reasons.

**Drainage for rainwater.** Water has always been a major problem in Jerusalem. In the entire city there is only one natural spring, and it is located at the foot of the City of David. It is called the Gihon Spring. Since Jerusalem has no rainfall for about seven or eight months per year, the residents have to collect it in the rainy season. The domed roofs allow all the rainwater to drain into waiting cisterns in the courtyard of the homes.

TYPICAL DOMED ROOF WITH DRAINS

**Inexpensive construction.** Poor people lived in the Old City for the most part. Roof beams are very expensive, since wood is scarce in this part of the world. So they would build the four walls, fill the room with soil, then mound it up to form a dome shape. Over this supporting mound they would lay the bricks for the roof. When the bricks had settled firmly, they then removed the dirt from the house, and what was left was what you see today, the domed roof.

I would like to recall a New Testament event that you can relate to from up here on the roof. Look all around the city and notice that there are many homes with connecting roofs. Perhaps this is what Jesus was looking at when he said the following. Matthew 24:17:

> Let him which is on the housetop not come down to take anything out of his house.

He was describing how to flee from the coming destruction, for it would be swift and terrible. Given the building patterns all around us, it is logical to assume that one could jump from roof to roof to flee the city.

EAST JERUSALEM FROM DOMED ROOFTOP

Before going back down into the courtyard, walk over to the LEFT side of the rear of the roof you are on. That very large complex of buildings is the Church of the Dormition. It is not on today's Walk, since it does not deal directly with Jesus' last week in Jerusalem. However, it is one of the very earliest Christian churches; a church has existed on this site since A.D. 130.

Now please go back down the stairway you came up. Once you have reached the courtyard with the large pine tree, find a comfortable place to sit down and do some reading. We are going to recall an event that may have taken place somewhere around here. It is the

## SITE OF PENTECOST (DESCENT OF THE HOLY SPIRIT)

Research shows that very early churches were built on the site now occupied by the Church of the Dormition. It is believed that this is the site where Jesus reappeared to his disciples and where the Holy Spirit descended.

After the Resurrection, Jesus appeared to Mary Magdalene and to two of his disciples as they were walking in the country. When they reported these appearances, they were not believed. Then one day, when all of the disciples except Thomas were gathered together in an upper room, suddenly Jesus appeared to them. John 20:21–22:

> Then said Jesus unto them again, Peace be with you: as my Father hath sent me, even so I send you
>
> And when he had said this, he breathed on them and saith unto them, Receive ye the Holy Ghost.

Thomas, told of this visit, doubted the word of his fellow disciples. John 20:25:

> Except I shall see in his hands the print of the nails, and put my finger into the print of the nails, and thrust my hand into his side, I will not believe.

This is how the expression "Doubting Thomas" originated. Eight days later, Thomas was also present when Jesus appeared. John 20:27–28:

> Then saith he to Thomas, Reach hither thy finger, and behold my hands, and reach hither thy hand, and thrust it into my side: and be not faithless, but believing.
>
> And Thomas answered and said unto him, My Lord and my God.

When the day of Pentecost had arrived, the disciples were gathered together in one place, and there was heard a sound from heaven and a mighty wind. Acts 2:3–4:

> And there appeared unto them cloven tongues, like as of fire, and it sat upon each of them:
>
> And they were all filled with the Holy Ghost, and began to speak with other tongues, as the Spirit gave them utterance.

The disciples were with foreigners who did not speak their language, since they came from many faraway countries. Suddenly each disciple began speaking in the language of the person next to him. At first the crowd thought that they were drunk and simply babbling away. Peter denied that they were drunk. Acts 2:15:

> For these are not drunken, as ye suppose, seeing it is but the third hour of the day.

Then Peter quoted the prophesy of Joel, the prophet. Acts 2:17:

> And it shall come to pass in the last days, saith God, I will pour out of my Spirit upon all flesh: and your sons and your daughters shall prophesy, and your young men shall see visions, and your old men shall dream dreams.

Word of the miracle of Speaking in Tongues spread, and that day three thousand were baptized in Jesus' name. On Walk 5 you will visit the most probable site of the mass baptism when we see the *Mikvot* (ritual baths) at the Southern Wall excavations. Now leave this courtyard by continuing ahead through the same arched overpath by which you entered a few minutes ago.

We are heading toward David's Tomb and the exit. I have made David's Tomb an optional stop if you so wish. Just follow the signs.

The Tomb is open Sunday through Thursday 8 A.M. to sunset, Friday 8 A.M. to 2 P.M. Closed Saturdays and Jewish Holidays.

## DAVID'S TOMB

Inside the inner room is a very large cenotaph (empty coffin or memorial). It is covered with a velvet cloth. I must point out that most scholars would describe this site as the "traditional" tomb of David, rather than the actual one. The Bible describes David's death very simply. I Kings 2:10:

> So David slept with his fathers, and was buried in the city of David.

This site became popular during the time of the Crusaders. The City of David is located outside the Old City on the Ophil Hill (South).

Now let's move along to the Cenacle, where we will recall the events that occurred at the Last Supper. Leave this building through the same door by which you entered. When you are back on the paved path, turn LEFT and continue ahead up the slope until you reach a set of steps. Turn LEFT here and walk along the

CENOTAPH OF DAVID

CENACLE OR ROOM OF THE LAST SUPPER

tiled path, and you will reach a large courtyard whose roof is made of branches. Cross the courtyard and walk up the stone steps, which are protected by an iron railing. At the top of the stairs you will enter an empty room. Walk through to the next room up ahead. This is the

## CENACLE OR COENACULUM (TRADITIONAL ROOM OF THE LAST SUPPER)

The Cenacle is open 8:30 A.M. to sundown, Sunday through Thursday; on Friday from 8:30 A.M. to 1 P.M.; closed Saturday and Jewish Holidays. Find a place to sit down. This is the ideal place to review the New Testament events that occurred here:

When the day of the feast arrived, Jesus sent Peter and John to locate a proper place and to prepare the meal. Luke 22: 8 and 12:

> And he sent Peter and John saying, Go and prepare us the passover that we may eat. . . .
>
> And he shall shew you a large upper room furnished: there make ready.

There is scholarly debate as to whether the Last Supper actually took place on the eve of the holiday of Passover or not. This argument is not within the scope of this book.

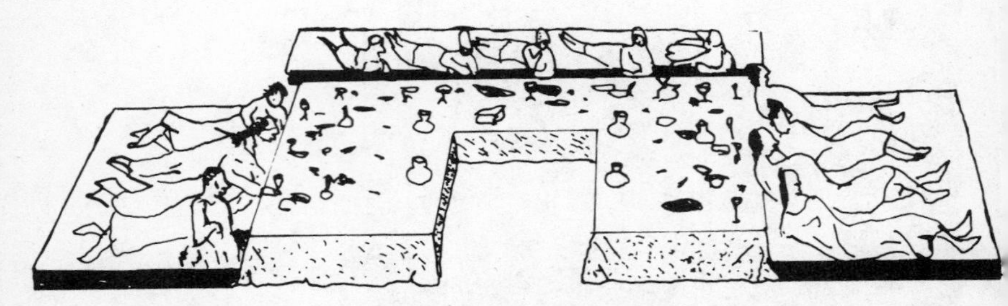

**SUGGESTED SEATING ARRANGEMENTS AT THE LAST SUPPER**

As pictured in the drawing above, the guests were probably seated, Roman fashion, around the *triclinium,* a dining table so arranged that guests sat on three sides, leaving the fourth open for service. The guests reclined on mats, which were laid on the floor. They supported themselves by resting on their left elbows, using their right hands to eat with. Food was served in communal bowls, which today is called family-style eating. The host of the evening (Jesus) may have assigned the places around the table to his guests, as it was customary for the host to do.

Jesus tells the disciples that this is his last meal with them. Luke 22:18:

> For I say unto you, I will not drink of the fruit of the vine, until the kingdom of God shall come.

Judas' betrayal is predicted. Luke 22:21:

> But, behold, the hand of him that betrayeth me is with me on the table.

The disciples asked each other who it could possibly be. Receiving no satisfactory reply they asked Jesus. Matthew 26:22–23:

> And they were exceedingly sorrowful, and began every one of them to say unto him, Lord is it I?
>
> And he answered and said, He that dippeth his hand with me in the dish, the same shall betray me.

Since Judas was the one who betrayed Jesus, I assume that he had to be seated very near to Jesus if he dipped his hand into the dish at the same time. It is probable that Judas was reclining next to and on the left side of Jesus. Matthew 26:25:

> Then Judas, which betrayed him, answered and said, Master is it I? He said unto him, Thou has said.

Then the following events occurred:

After the blessing of the bread, Jesus divided it among his disciples. Matthew 26:26:

> Take, eat; this is my body.

After he blessed the wine, he said, Matthew 26:28:

> For this is my blood of the new testament, which is shed for many for the remission of sins.

Jesus washed the disciples feet. John 13:5:

> After that he poureth water into a bason, and began to wash the disciples feet, and to wipe them with the towel wherewith he was girded.

He then explained to them that he, whom they called Lord and master, had humbled himself by the act of washing their feet in order to teach them humility. John 13:14:

> If I then, your Lord and Master, have washed your feet: ye also ought to wash one another's feet.

At the conclusion of the Last Supper, they all sang the traditional hymns, Psalms 115 through 118. The meal finished, they left Mount Zion and went down to the Garden of Gethsemane, where after a night of prayer, Jesus was betrayed by Judas and arrested.

Now let's look around the room. This room measures 30 by 50 feet. It was part of a fourth-century church, the Haga Sion. In A.D. 614, it was destroyed by the Persians and was rebuilt by the Crusaders in A.D. 1099. It is the remains of the Crusader church that you see today.

Does anything seem out of character for a Christian shrine? Yes, there are obvious traces of the Muslim past—with Arabic writing and other architectual impositions. This all occurred after Islam ousted the Crusaders, and Christian sites were reused by the Muslims. Christians were forbidden to enter this room. It was turned into a mosque.

An interesting observation is that this one particular building on Mount Zion is revered by the Jews (David's Tomb), the Christians (the Cenacle), and the Muslims (Jesus is recognized as a prophet by Islam).

## Crusader Remains

The columns in this room are all Crusader. We can positively date them to the Crusader period through the beautiful capitals atop each column. The ceiling is likewise Crusader in design. Take a position as if you were first entering the room and walk to the RIGHT hand corner toward the small gray stone column ahead, which is supporting an arched canopy over a staircase.

**PELICAN COLUMN**

Notice that images of pelicans have been incised into the capital. This Byzantine or Crusader capital depicts two young pelicans feeding off the blood of their mother. This symbolizes that Jesus sacrificed himself for his followers. Now, please move to the center of the room and concentrate on the rear wall.

## Muslim Alterations

This room was built by the Crusaders. The Muslims kept the existing Gothic-style windows but replaced the glass panes with Islamic designs. On the wall is a blue ceramic plaque with quotes from the Koran. In the center of the room there is a niche in the wall; this is called a *mihrab*.

MIHRAB OR MUSLIM PRAYER NICHE

It is a Muslim prayer niche, which is built into every place of prayer. It faces in the direction of Mecca, the holiest of all Muslim cities. In this room it faces south, which is the direction of Mecca from Jerusalem.

We have now completed our tour of the Cenacle. Leave this area by retracing your steps all the way back down to the road,

**CROSS AND COCK ATOP SAINT PETER IN GALLICANTU CHURCH**

which means we will pass the Chamber of the Holocaust and David's Tomb on the way out.

When you reach the main road, look both ways for the traffic and then cross the road and turn LEFT going up the hill. Walk until you reach the driveway on the RIGHT. It's about a three-minute walk. You will see a sign reading "Private Road, No Thoroughfare." Turn in here and begin walking down the road. We are heading for the Church of Saint Peter in Gallicantu, which is located down below at the bottom of this road, about a five-minute walk. As you walk down, from time to time you will get a glimpse of the roof of the church. When you get close enough, notice that one of the roofs has not only a cross on top but a rooster as well. This is the theme of the church. The word Gallicantu means a "rooster crowing." This church commemorates Peter's denial of Jesus and his redemption. Matthew 26:74:

> Then began he [Peter] to curse and to swear, saying, I know not the man [Jesus]. And immediately the cock crew.

Now continue down the road, and in the open space which is a parking area, walk ahead to the low stone wall, overlooking the valley below. This is the Hinnom Valley where the following event took place:

## ACELDAMA, THE FIELD OF BLOOD

After Judas had learned that the Romans had condemned Jesus to death by crucifixion he returned the thirty pieces of silver he had received for betraying him to the Temple authorities. Matthew 27:4 and 5:

> Saying, I have sinned in that I have betrayed the innocent blood. . . .
>
> And he cast down the pieces of silver in the temple, and departed, and went and hanged himself.

But the money that Judas returned was considered to be blood money and couldn't be returned to the Temple Treasury. Matthew 27:7 and Acts 1:19:

> And they took counsel, and bought with them [the pieces of silver] the potter's field to bury strangers in.
>
> And it was known unto all the dwellers of Jerusalem; in so much as that field is called in their proper tongue, Aceldama, that is to say, The field of blood.

Let's continue on. Turn around and follow the road down the hill bearing to your RIGHT. We are not going to enter the church just yet, but as you approach, notice the mosaic on the outside of the building.

### Exterior of Saint Peter in Gallicantu Church

**On the side of the building.** We see a representation of Jesus bound with a rope harness and seemingly being lowered down. The last stop on today's walk will lead us to a maximum security cell into which we believe many prisoners were likewise lowered. Continue ahead, and on the front of the church is another mosaic.

**Over the entrance.** We see Jesus with his hands bound. It alludes to his hearing before High Priest Caiaphas. Now continue down the staircase and head for the high green fence ahead. Enter the Archaeological Site from the end gate in the fence.

CHURCH EXTERIOR FROM ARCHAEOLOGICAL SITE

MOSAIC, JESUS BEING LOWERED INTO A PIT

## ARCHAEOLOGICAL SITE

Ahead is an ancient rock-cut stairway. Walk over and sit down on it, for we are going to spend a few minutes getting acquainted with this entire site.

### Background to the Site

We will deal with three major events during Jesus' last week in Jerusalem:

- His hearing before High Priest Caiaphas.
- Possibility of his having been held in a prison overnight.
- Peter's denial and repentance.

At the moment of his arrest, Jesus instructed all of his disciples to flee. The guards then took Jesus from the Garden of Gethsemane to the house of High Priest Caiaphas, which is believed to have been located somewhere on Mount Zion. Matthew 26:57:

> And they that had laid hold on Jesus led him away to Caiaphas the high priest.

Many scholars disagree on its actual location. Some believe that it is here at Saint Peter in Gallicantu, and others feel strongly that it is in the Armenian Garden farther up on Mount Zion. The only point on which most agree is that it was probably on Mount Zion.

### The Ancient Staircase

These stairs may be one of the most important sites you will visit on these walks. They existed in Jesus' day. We are certain of this because the archaeologists discovered a coin from the Hasmonaean period (Maccabees) between the cracks of the stairs. This predates Jesus by about 150 years. Thus it is very possible that Jesus himself walked up this staircase, which runs from the Cenacle to the Pool of Siloam.

STAIRCASE THAT PREDATES JESUS BY AT LEAST A CENTURY

After being arrested down below in the Garden of Gethsemane, he may have been led down through the Kidron Valley below, and up to Caiaphas' house on Mount Zion by these stairs. They are the way people climbed up to Mount Zion in Jesus' day. Surely worth a picture or two of you standing on the same steps.

Now let's go down below to the excavations themselves. As you descend the ancient stairs, stop next to the high green fence on the LEFT. You are looking at

## The Remains of a Roman Bath Complex

Try to picture the baths as they were in Jesus' time.

REMAINS OF BATH COMPLEX

**The Cisterns.** Walk over to the caves on the LEFT. These water storage caves (cisterns) provided the water for the baths. They were filled with rainwater running down the mountain. Notice that they still have some of the ancient plaster on the walls inside. Now look on the other side of the fence at

**The Very Wide Entrance Steps.** The fact that these steps were plastered tells us that the water level probably reached the top step. That's how deep the pool was.

**A Heated Pool.** The archaeologists found remains of an oven that was made of red bricks. The water coming into the pool was heated when it passed over the hot bricks.

Another interesting thing to consider is the location of the baths. Most Orthodox Jews were against accepting anything that was of Greek influence, such as theaters, gymnasiums, chariot racing in the hippodrome, or Roman-style bath houses. But the high priests, appointed by the ruling Roman governors, were Hellenized Jews, who enjoyed Greek cultural niceties. Thus the existence of baths here hints that this house may be linked to a priestly family.

Now continue on down the hill, and stop when you are in line with the double row of pine trees on the LEFT. This is a possible site of

## The Roman Theater

On the next walk you will see a model of the theater at the Holyland Hotel. Its exact location within the city is still a mystery. However airphotos of this site show some evidence that a theater may have existed here. From the air we can see an outline in a circular design. It is hoped that, in the near future, new excavations will start on this site.

Walk down to the dirt path on the RIGHT. Follow this path for about thirty steps. You have arrived at the industrial complex. This complex was part of a large estate. There is evidence here that they had their own bakery to supply a large household and staff with fresh bread on a daily basis.

GRINDING STONE

You should be standing in an area where large sections of rock have been chiseled to a flat surface. Look down BELOW, and you will see a large round stone in the center of what was once a room. These are the remains of a grinding stone. Near it is the storage silo.

### A Cistern

The steps leading down into this rock-cut cistern are in bad shape, so please don't try to go down. Notice the remains of the ancient plastering.

Now we are finished on this site and are heading up to the church. The easiest way up is to return to the path by the silo and continue in the direction that takes you away from the ancient stairway. Once on top there is a staircase with an iron railing; it is painted black. Leave this site by the stairs on the LEFT, and notice the many other ancient remains as you walk along.

## SAINT PETER IN GALLICANTU CHURCH

Once on top, walk to the entrance of the church, but don't go inside just yet. Look at the snack bar opposite you across the road. I want you to look at the large stone over the doorway. This is

## The Korban Inscription Stone

The inscription on this stone has now faded so that it cannot be seen today. But you can see the inscription in a photograph that was taken when it was first found. The Hebrew word *Korban* means "sacrifice." (See Mark 7:11.) Sacrifice at the temple was the form that prayer took in Jesus' time. The fact that this stone was found on this property is evidence that a priestly family lived here.

Let's now go inside the church itself. If the door is locked, push the red button, and a priest will admit you. Once inside, stop in the vestibule and look at

## The Showcase on the Wall

Inside are artifacts and photographs of some of the more important archaeological finds made on this site. First of all look at the photograph of the stone with the *Korban* inscription, which we just saw outside. Next look at the photos of the dry and liquid weights. The significance of these weights is that similar weights have been found in Jewish Quarter excavations in the homes of priests from this same period of history. One of the priests' responsibilities was to settle disputes between merchants, who were accused of cheating a storekeeper.

Now walk straight into the church through the doors ahead. The church is open every day except Sunday, 8:30 to 11:45 A.M., 2 to 5:30 P.M. It is also closed on January 1, June 29, August 15, November 1, and December 25, all solemn feast days.

## The Upper Church

Rather than commemorate Peter's denial of Jesus, Architect Boubet chose to represent Peter's repentence. This is carried out by the dominant blues and greens, the colors of the "new life."

**INTERIOR OF THE UPPER CHURCH**

Please go over and take a seat on one of the back pews. Let's now review the events to which this church is dedicated. Mark 14:30:

> And Jesus saith unto him, Verily I say unto thee, That this day, even in this night, before the cock crow twice, thou shall deny me thrice.

When Jesus was taken to Caiaphas' house, Peter followed and went in and sat with the servants. Matthew 26:69–75:

> Now Peter sat without in the palace; and a damsel came unto him, saying, Thou also wast with Jesus of Galilee.
>
> But he denied before them all, saying, I know not what thou sayest.
>
> And when he was gone out into the porch, another maid saw him, and said unto them that were there, This fellow was also with Jesus of Nazareth.

> And again he denied with an oath, I do not know the man.
>
> And after a while came unto him they that stood by, and said to Peter, Surely thou also art one of them: for thy speech bewrayeth thee. [The Jews of Galilee had a recognizable accent.]
>
> Then began he to curse and to swear, saying, I know not the man. And immediately the cock crew.
>
> And Peter remembered the word of Jesus, which said unto him, Before the cock crow, thou shalt deny me thrice. And he went out, and wept bitterly.

It is important to keep in mind that, unlike Judas who, after betraying Jesus, despaired and took his own life, Peter redeemed himself. Calling on an inner strength, he found a new life through repentence and forgiveness and became a leader in the early Church. This is what the architect chose to represent in this church.

The other event in Jesus' last week in Jerusalem that we will explore in this church is Matthew 26:57:

> And they that had laid hold on Jesus led him away to Caiaphas the high priest.

Shortly we will go below, where, on the lowest level of this church, is what appears to be a prison and a maximum-security cell. But first, at this level, let us observe the magnificent mosaics.

## The Wall Mosaics

Begin with the first mosaic to the LEFT of the entrance.

**Mosaic 1, upper panel.** Jesus, having been tried and convicted of blasphemy, is being led to the prison below. As he passes through the courtyard, he meets Peter, who begins to cry. Notice the Roman soldiers on the left, who have built a fire in the courtyard to keep warm on this chilly spring evening in Jerusalem.

**Mosaic 1, lower panel.** A mature Peter, his left hand resting on the keys to the kingdom of heaven.

**Mosaic 2, left side of altar.** Three male sinners have repented, including one of the convicted criminals who is to be crucified with Jesus. The writings around the mosaics are events as they were recorded in the diaries of some early pilgrims to the Holy Land.

**Mosaic 3, behind altar.** The trial of Jesus by High Priest Caiaphas and the members of the Sanhedrin.

**Mosaic 4, right side of the altar.** Three women sinners who have repented.

As you go toward the rear of the church, you will see

**Mosaic 5, lower panel.** John the Evangelist.

**Mosaic 5, upper panel.** The Last Supper.

**Mosaic 6, rear wall.** Mary, mother of Jesus.

Now look up at the stained-glass cross.

CEILING OF SAINT PETER IN GALLICANTU CHURCH

What a magnificent ceiling decoration. If you remember, during the trial Caiaphas asked Jesus if he was the Son of God. Matthew 26:64:

> Jesus saith unto him, Thou has said: Nevertheless I say unto you, Hereafter shall you see the Son of man sitting on the right hand of power, and coming in the clouds of heaven.

Look at the center of the cross carefully, and you will see Jesus "coming in the clouds of heaven." The twelve angels running around the dome represent the twelve apostles and the twelve tribes of Israel. Now please get up and walk toward the front of the church and notice the large display map on the right. If you care to, you can purchase a copy of this map on the way out. Now head for the door on the LEFT in the front of this church. This leads us to

## A Viewing Platform of the Excavations Below

Here we have a marvelous overview of the excavations we walked through a little while ago. From this spot it is possible to get the

EXCAVATION SITE

full visual effect of the possible path that Jesus was led on after his arrest in the Garden of Gethsemane and then brought up here on Mount Zion to the House of Caiaphas.

If they did indeed take this route, then it would be safe to say that Jesus did indeed actually walk up this stairway.

When you are ready, leave this platform the same way you entered. Walk to the rear of the church and out the doors. We are going below to the area commonly referred to as the Common Prison and Maximum Security Cell.

As soon as you enter the vestibule of the church turn RIGHT, and go through the door, which will take you downstairs. When you reach the first landing, notice the Byzantine mosaic floor, which has been restored on the landing. This is part of the original church that stood on this site. When you reach the next floor, notice that the light coming through the stained-glass windows has an extraordinary glow. Its purpose is to reflect the "new life." Sit down on the bench on the LEFT and let's do some readings prior to going down to view the Prison.

## THE COMMON PRISON

After Jesus had declared himself the Son of Man, the following events took place. Matthew 26:65:

> Then the high priest rent his clothes [a sign of mourning], saying: He hath spoken blasphemy, what further need have we of witnesses? behold, now ye have heard his blasphemy.

The guards then led Jesus out into the courtyard, where he saw Peter. Could they then have led him down into the prison to await a hearing by Pontius Pilate in the morning? Let us go down to the site of the putative prison, which the priests of this church call the Place of the Scourging.

Continue down the next two staircases, and on the LEFT is the gate leading to the Common Prison. If the gate is locked, ask the father for the key.

There is some speculation among Israeli archaeologists that this might actually have been an Israelite house (1000–586 B.C.).

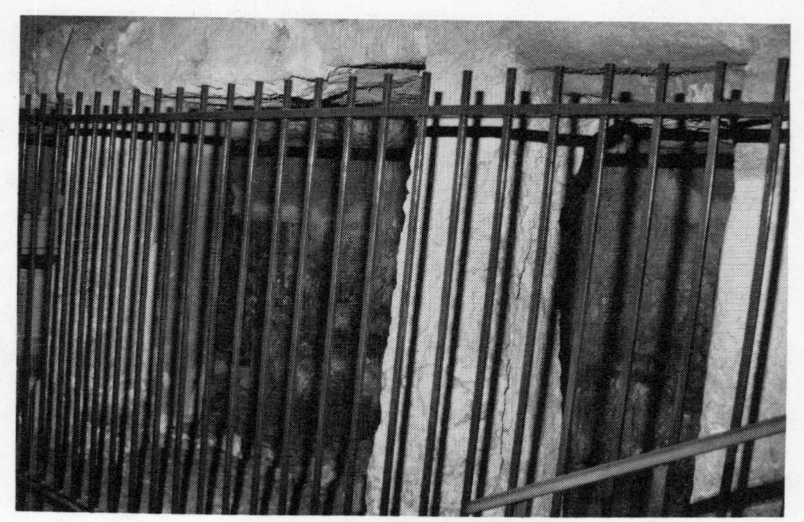

**VIEW OF ANCIENT PRISON**

However most archaeologists feel that the floor is too rough for a family home, and there are many signs that point to a prison. Let's examine the room on your RIGHT first.

## The Place of the Scourging

One of the more common forms of punishment was whipping or, as they called it, scourging. A prisoner would be stripped, then hung by his hands to a pillar and whipped. As he began to bleed, his wounds would be sponged with brine ("pouring salt into the wounds") and then again with water.

Above the entrance to this room, the stone has been chipped away in two places in a curious manner—a good place to string up a bound prisoner. Secondly, a pillar is missing, which once was close to the entrance. On either side of the entrance, the stone has been chipped away, and what remains is in effect two bowls. Could this have been for the brine and water?

Now cross the room and go into the LEFT section. A metal staircase will take you into this area. Once inside, head for the window in the wall. Look DOWN at the step under the window.

Step up and look through the window. What you are seeing is what many believe to be

## A Maximum Security Cell (the Pit)

First of all, notice that the stone you are now standing on was not placed here. It is part of the original bedrock of this floor. In order to make this step, they had to chip away the entire floor area surrounding it. I consider that good evidence that they purposely located this step under the window so that a guard could keep an eye on the prisoner below.

To reach the pit, walk back up the stairs, and when you reach the top of the short stone staircase, walk STRAIGHT AHEAD. Pass the staircase going up and continue to the door on the RIGHT. Walk down, and you are entering the Maximum Security Cell.

STAIRS DOWN TO THE PIT

## Crosses Painted on the Walls

You will have to look very carefully to find them all. There are eleven painted crosses and three incised. Unfortunately their exposure to the air has caused most of them to fade quite a bit.

Now, if indeed this was the actual dungeon where they held Jesus overnight, imagine the lonely night he spent. Arrested, accused of blasphemy, deserted by his disciples, and denied by one of his most beloved disciples, Jesus most likely turned to prayer. Could the following verses have gone through his head as he prayed? Psalm 8: verses 1, 3, 4, 6, and 8:

> O Lord, God of my salvation I have cried day and night before thee.
>
> For my soul is full of troubles, and my life draweth nigh unto the grave.
>
> I am counted with them that go down into the pit: I am as a man that hath no strength.
>
> Thou hast laid me in the lowest pit in darkness, in the deeps.
>
> Thou hast put away mine acquaintance far from me: thou hast made me an abomination unto them: I am shut up, and I cannot come forth.

When you are ready to leave here, go back up the stairs and turn LEFT. Look down into the Pit from the round hole cut into the rock, and notice the Byzantine cross incised around the opening. Turn LEFT again, and follow the staircase up, and it will lead you out of the church.

The snack bar opposite the church has clean rest rooms, and you might want something to refresh yourself by now. If you brought the picnic lunch I suggested, then walk to the RIGHT out of the church, and on the LEFT a little ways up you will see a green area with large shade trees. Enjoy your lunch.

## GETTING BACK TO THE CITY

By now you may be a bit tired. So rather than direct you up the steep winding hill from which we entered this site, I suggest that you turn RIGHT, leaving the church, and take the path all the way (a ten-minute walk), which will end at the Dung Gate. From here you can get a bus or taxi back to the city.

**By Bus to West Jerusalem.** Outside the Dung Gate, and straight ahead is the stop for the No. 1 bus, which will take you directly into West Jerusalem.

**By Bus to East Jerusalem.** Do not enter the Dung Gate. Walk along down the steep hill and on the RIGHT side of the road. At the first cross street, cross over and wait for the bus with the Arabic markings. There are no official bus stops so just signal the driver, and he will stop for you. It goes to the Damascus Gate bus terminal.

**By Taxi.** Opposite the Dung Gate is a taxi stand.

## THE NEXT WALK

First of all I suggest that you take a lunch break between Walks if you are doing two a day. The next Walk is at the Holyland Hotel in West Jerusalem. It is the Model of Jerusalem in A.D. 66.

Timewise you have no problem, since the Model is open all day from 8 A.M. to 5 P.M. It's a little out of town, so if you can afford it, take a taxi about a two- to three-dollar ride from the Dung Gate. If you prefer a bus, take the No. 1 into the Central Bus Station and transfer to the No. 21 bus, which stops at the Holyland Hotel. For directions to the Model once you get off the No. 21 bus, see the next walk's instructions.

WALK

# 4

# *The Scale Model of Jerusalem in* A.D. *66*

Today's tour goal is to use this realistic Scale Model of the city to recall various New Testament events and to familiarize you with the way Jerusalem looked to Jesus. We will see what a central role was played in the drama of Jesus' ministry by the Second Temple of Herod the Great, to prepare you for the last two climactic walks, which take place in and near the Temple Mount.

## GETTING TO THE STARTING POINT

Today's tour begins and ends at the Holyland Hotel in West Jerusalem, where the Scale Model is located.

**By Bus from West Jerusalem.** Take the Egged bus No. 21. Pick it up anywhere on Jaffa Road or at the Central Bus Station. The starting point is less than half an hour from the center of Jerusalem. Once off the bus, turn RIGHT, walking down the hill. Go past the main entrance of the Holyland Hotel, down the hill, and keep walking until you see a sign on the LEFT directing you to the Model.

**By Bus from East Jerusalem.** There are no direct buses to the Model. So we suggest that you come into West Jerusalem and catch the No. 21 Egged bus.

OVERVIEW OF MODEL

**By Car.** From the center of town, drive down King George Street. Take a RIGHT on Ramban Street. Then your first LEFT. Drive down two blocks and make a right on Aza Road. Drive straight out Aza Road. In about ten minutes, you will see a sign halfway up a steep hill directing you to the Model. There is a parking lot across from the entrance to the Model.

**By Taxi.** About a fifteen-minute ride from town.

## THE SCALE MODEL FACT SHEET

The Model represents Jerusalem about thirty years or so after Jesus' death.

### Facts

**Built.** As a visual aid for the teaching of future generations.

**Size.** 800 square meters.

**Time period.** A.D. 66.

**Conceived and designed.** By Prof. Michael Avi-Yonah, Department of Archaeology, Hebrew University, Jerusalem.

**Construction.** Begun in 1964, completed in 1970.

**Accuracy.** Several sites are inconsistent with the facts as we know them today, because most of the Scale Model was completed before 1967, when Israeli archaeologists did not have access to the Old City.

**Sources used.** The Mishna, Josephus, synagogue mosaics, oral tradition, Philo, the New Testament, and representations on coins.

**Materials Used.** Same as in the original city: hard limestone, chalk, bronze, copper, gold, and wood.

**Topography.** The model closely follows the topography of the original city. As an example, when rainfall hits the Model, it runs off into the same valleys as it does today in the real city.

**Scale of Model.** ¼ inch equals 1 foot. At our first stop, I will demonstrate a good way to judge the relationship of the buildings on the Model to their real-life counterparts. The Psephinus Tower is shown as 2 feet 3½ inches tall. It represents a tower that was actually 115 feet in height. The actual scale of the model is 1 to 50.

**Buildings on Model.** Designed by Eva Avi-Yonah, the wife of Professor Avi-Yonah.

**Visiting Hours.** 8 A.M. to 5 P.M. daily, including Saturday. There is a small entrance fee.

The Temple Mount, the most holy area in the city, was a very complex structure. The Temple itself played the central role in the spiritual, social, and cultural life of the Jews of that day. There is no doubt that Jesus, being a man of his times, was greatly influenced by the Temple.

The Model shows three walls encircling the city. The outermost wall (the one closest to you at the Model) is called the third wall. It did not exist in Jesus' day. This entire area was unwalled and sparsely populated. I have included the line drawing below to clarify the situation.

THIRD WALL AS SHOWN ON THE MODEL

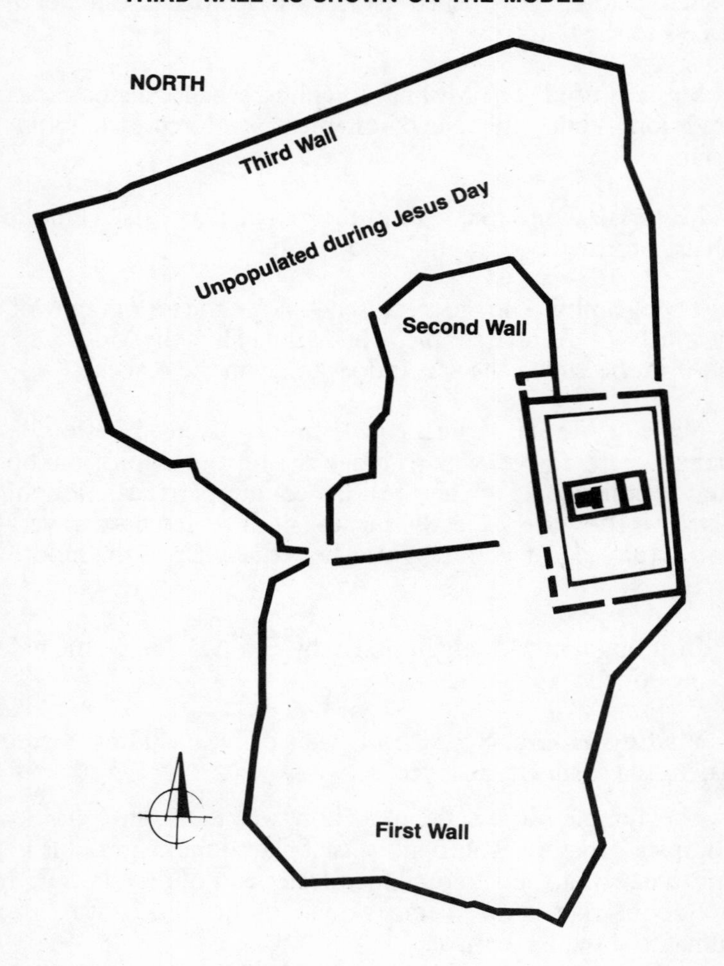

## STOPS WE WILL MAKE AT THE MODEL

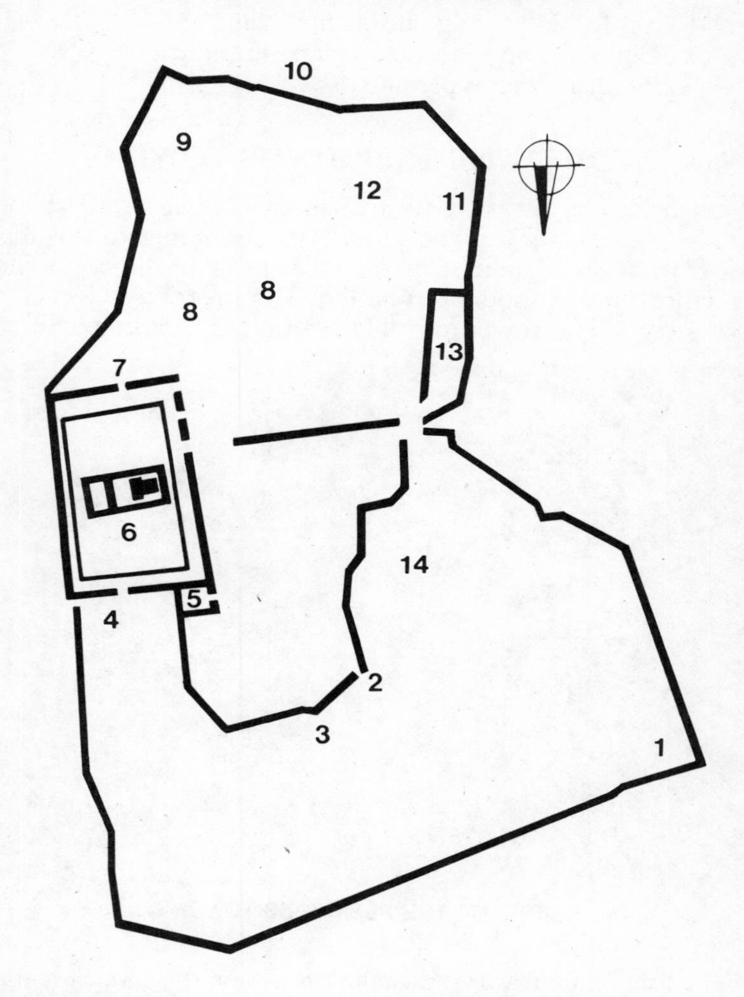


1. Psephinus Tower
2. Damascus Gate
3. Garden Tomb
4. Bethesda Pools
5. Antonia Fortress
6. Temple Mount
7. Southern Wall
8. Hippodrome/Theater
9. Pool of Siloam
10. Aceldama
11. House of Caiaphas
12. David's Tomb
13. King Herod's Palace
14. Golgotha (Calvary)

*Please observe the rules:*

1. It is forbidden to go inside the chain.
2. Use of movie and video cameras forbidden.
3. Regular cameras permitted.

## STOP 1: THE PSEPHINUS TOWER

Once inside the entrance, turn to the RIGHT and stop at the Tower in the corner of the Model. We are going to use this Tower to help you understand the relationship of the size of the structures in this model to real life. The model is 2 feet 3½ inches high. The Tower in real life stood 115 feet in height.

MODEL OF THE PSEPHINUS TOWER

The Psephinus Tower is the tallest tower on this model. It was built as a lookout tower, sort of an early warning system against any enemy armies advancing on Jerusalem from the north. The north has always been the weak side of Jerusalem, and every successful attack on the city has come from that direction. The other three sides are protected by very steep valleys, while the north is a plateau.

Now, turn to your LEFT and begin walking. Take about seventeen steps, stop, and look into the model. Find the Damascus Gate.

## STOP 2: THE DAMASCUS GATE

**MODEL OF GATE IN THE SECOND WALL**

Looking at the second wall, you will see an entrance gate; this is where today's Damascus Gate is located. I am using it as a reference point to help you orient yourself to the modern city. Today you would be standing in what is called East Jerusalem. I hope this helps you to get your bearings.

Now we are going to locate the site of the Garden Tomb.

## STOP 3: THE GARDEN TOMB (GORDON'S CALVARY)

Notice the gate with wide Towers on each side (in the second wall). Straight in FRONT of you and about two feet to the RIGHT is an outcropping of rock with some vegetation. This is the site of the Garden Tomb today.

**MODEL OF THE GARDEN TOMB SITE**

This area was popularized as a possible site of Calvary by British General C. G. ("Chinese") Gordon, a devout Christian who spent a year in the Holy Land in 1883. He felt that this region matched the Biblical description of Calvary better than the Holy Sepulcher Church site. On the last walk in this book we will visit the Garden Tomb and discuss his theory in more detail.

Our next stop is the Bethesda Pools. Continue along in the same direction you have been walking, and stop when you are OPPOSITE the tall building with the four towers. This is the Antonia Fortress. We will discuss it in a moment. But now turn your attention to the double pool just to the RIGHT of and below the Antonia Fortress.

## STOP 4: THE BETHESDA POOLS (THE SHEEP POOLS)

The Bethesda Pools are mentioned only once in the New Testament. John 5:2–3:

> Now there is at Jerusalem by the sheep market, a pool, which is called in the Hebrew tongue Bethesda, having five porches.
>
> In these pools lay a great multitude of impotent folk, of blind, halt, withered, waiting for the moving of the water.

**MODEL OF THE BETHESDA POOLS**

John relates that some Jerusalemites believed that at a certain season an angel came down and stirred up the waters. Whichever of the crippled was the first to enter the water was cured of his affliction. One man had been waiting for thirty-eight years to be cured. He was lame and had no one to help him enter the water so he never got there before the others. Jesus spoke to him and asked him if he wanted to be cured. He said yes. John 5:8–9:

> Jesus saith unto him, Rise, take up thy bed, and walk
>
> And immediately the man was made whole, and took up his bed, and walked.

Just behind the Bethesda Pools is

## STOP 5: ANTONIA FORTRESS

The Model shows a fortress that overlooks the Temple Mount itself. This four-towered structure was where the Roman legions,

**MODEL OF THE ROMAN FORTRESS**

whose responsibility it was to maintain order on the Mount, were quartered. There is a long-standing tradition that the Judgment of Jesus by the Roman Governor Pontius Pilate may have taken place nearby. Matthew: 27:2 and 11:

> And when they had bound him, they led him away, and delivered him to Pontius Pilate, the governor.
>
> And Jesus stood before the governor: and the governor asked him, saying: Are thou the King of the Jews? And Jesus said unto him, Thou sayest.

We will be visiting the ruins of the Antonia Fortress on the next walk and will wait until then to review the events that followed the sentencing of Jesus by Pilate.

## STOP 5: THE TEMPLE MOUNT

Move a few feet to your left, and you should be standing in FRONT of the Temple. It is a large white-marble building trimmed in gold. Notice that it is sitting on a platform. This is called the Temple Mount.

The Model shows the Temple and its surrounding structures more or less as they appeared in Jesus' day. The basic design was that of a central building (Temple) surrounded on all sides by a series of courts or courtyards. Each court was restricted to a certain group of people, who were not permitted to penetrate farther into the sacred precincts. For the full details of the Temple Mount and its various courts, see pages 19–35.

MODEL OF THE TEMPLE MOUNT

## THE COURT LAYOUT

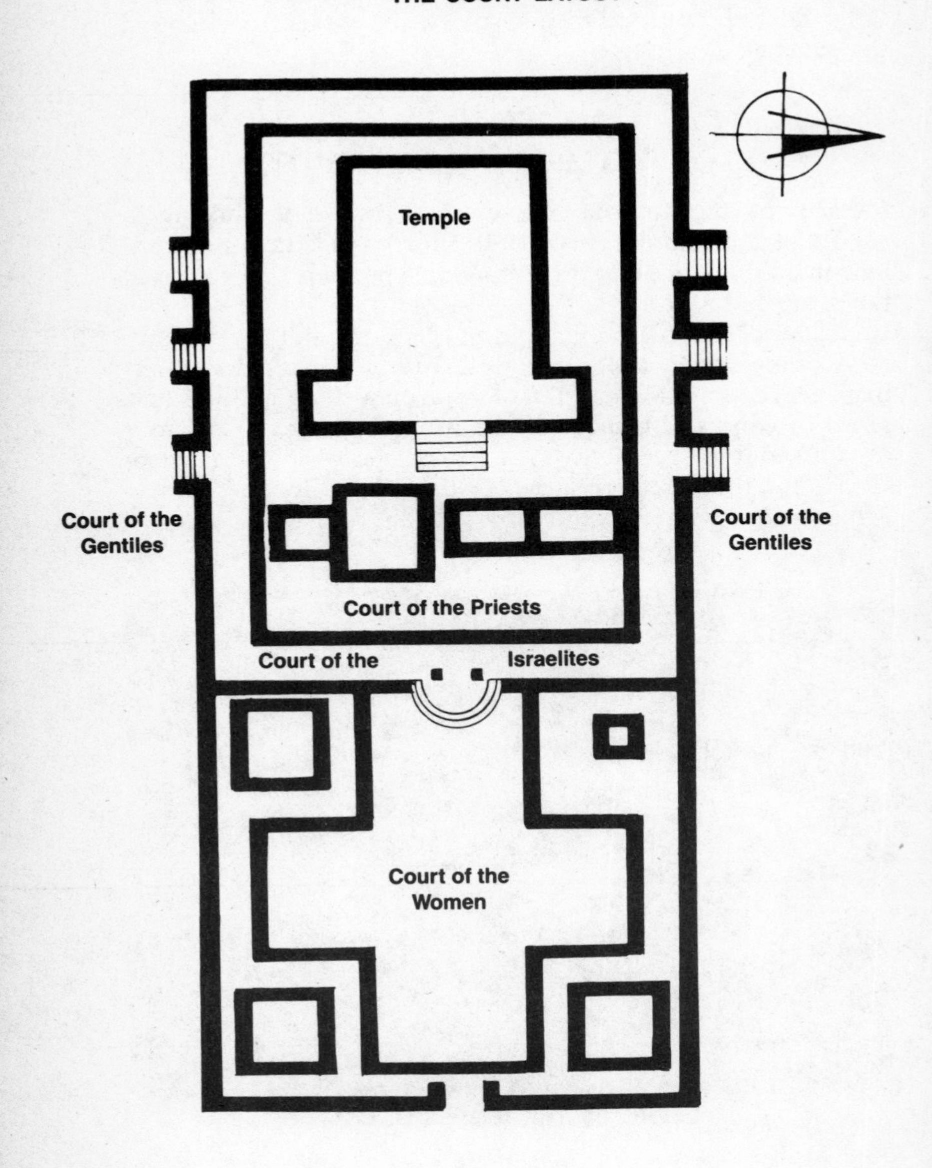

Unfortunately the Model is positioned in such a way that you will not be able to see all the inner courts clearly. So use the drawing (opposite) for your reference points.

Several New Testament events concerning Jesus, Paul, and Peter are believed to have occurred in and around the Temple Mount.

Surrounding the inner courts was a screened wall called the Balustrade or *Soreg*. Non-Jews were forbidden to pass through this wall into the Temple court on pain of immediate death. Signs were posted to that effect in Greek and Latin. Paul was accused of taking two non-Jews past the balustrade. (See page 186.)

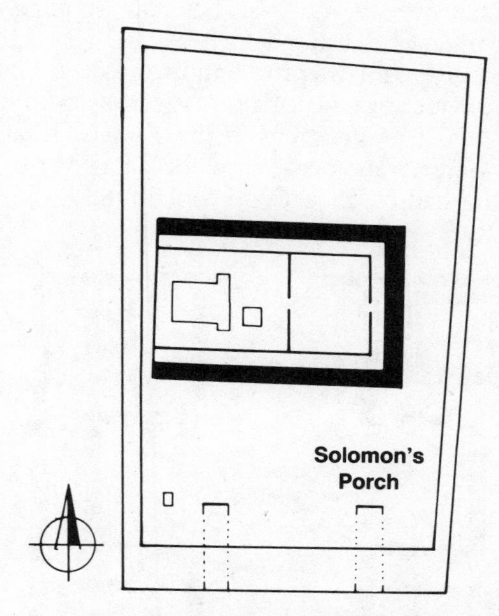


**LOCATION OF SOLOMON'S PORCH**

The Balustrade in above diagram is shown by a dark line. Look into the Model and locate the Balustrade, which is represented by chips of stone.

## Solomon's Porch

Jesus visited the Temple during the winter Feast of the Dedication (Chanukah). John 10:22–23:

> And it was at Jerusalem the feast of the dedication, and it was winter.
>
> And Jesus walked in the temple in Solomon's porch.

It was commonly believed that Solomon's Porch was located on the southeastern side of the Mount and had been constructed by King Solomon when he built the First Temple.

## The Beautiful Gate

Peter's encounter with the crippled beggar (see page 180) took place near the Beautiful Gate, which as you can see from the drawing (opposite page) was the entrance to the Court of the Women. There were money coffers (collection boxes) there for those who wanted to contribute to the Temple Treasury. Thus the Beautiful Gate is an ideal place for a beggar to sit, since everyone passing had coins ready to contribute.

THE BEAUTIFUL GATE

## The Court of the Women

As mentioned above, the Court of the Women also served as the Treasury, where pilgrims came to make a donation to the Temple. It was probably here that the incident of the Widow's Mite took place. (See page 181.)

MODEL OF THE TEMPLE

Many of the people who heard Jesus predict the destruction of the Temple may have had their doubts about his prophecy. The Temple itself was seventeen stories high and was constructed of stone—certainly a very formidable and sturdy building. Yet a mere forty years later it was totally destroyed, just as Jesus predicted. Matthew 24:2 and 21:

> And Jesus said unto them, See ye not all these things? Verily I say unto you, There shall not be left here one stone upon another, that shall not be thrown down.
>
> For then shall be great tribulation, such as was not since the beginning of the world to this time, no, nor ever shall be.

The temple was probably the strongest building in Jerusalem. Yet the Romans in A.D. 70 completely destroyed it. How did they do it?

You will recall that on Walk 2 in the Garden of Gethsemane we learned that the Romans cut down all the trees within a twelve-mile radius of Jerusalem, then used the logs to lean against the walls of the city and Temple and set them afire. Once the heat caused the limestone to steam up and explode, the Romans then took battering rams and iron rods and knocked all the stones down.

Now let's move a few steps to the LEFT and line up with the two-storied multicolumned portico. This was known as the

## Royal Stoa

This great portico was 900 feet long and 137 feet high, and contained 162 columns, each 27 feet high, as described by Josephus in *Antiquities*. It is believed that the incident of the Roman coins took place in or near the Royal Stoa. (See page 176.)

## The Chaniyot (Shops or Stalls)

It seems that there was a commercial shopping center *(Chaniyot)* somewhere in the vicinity of the Temple Mount. Its function was to provide the pilgrims with the items they needed on their visit to the Mount, such as sacrificial birds and animals and proper coinage for donations.

ROYAL STOA

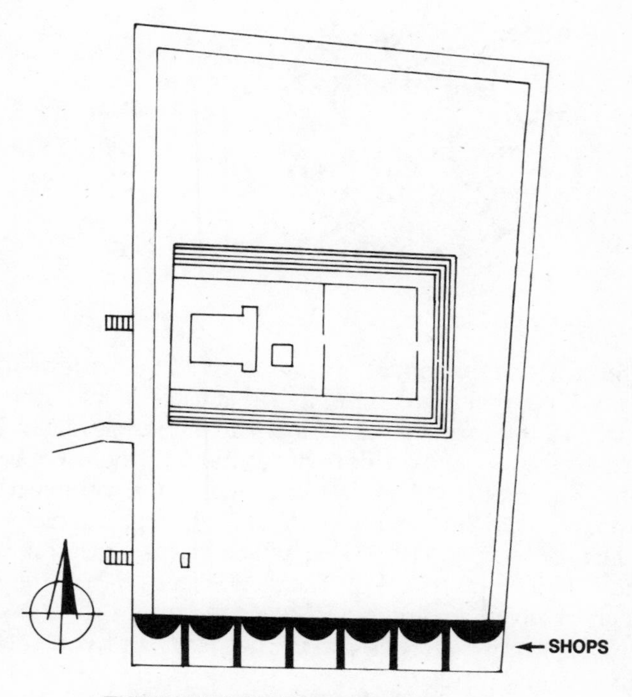


THE CHANIYOT (SHOPS OR STALLS)

There is some feeling that these shops may have been located within the Royal Stoa. Matthew 21:12:

> And Jesus went into the temple of God, and cast out all of them that sold and bought in the temple, and overthrew the tables of the moneychangers and the seats of them that sold doves.

It is logical to assume that Jesus disapproved of commerce being conducted so close to the Temple itself. But doves were used as sacrificial birds by women, and the money changers were performing a function made necessary by the Second Commandment, Exodus 20:4:

> Thou shall not make unto thee any graven images.

**PAGAN COIN**

This Biblical commandment was interpreted by the Jews to mean that anything that God himself had created could not be reproduced in any form by man. Since the pilgrims came to Jerusalem from all over the world, they naturally brought coins which bore the image of Greek gods and Roman emperors. These coins were unacceptable in the Temple Treasury, so pagan coins had to be exchanged for Jewish coins, which had only floral or geometrical designs inscribed on them. For this service, the money changers received a commission.

Now let's move a few steps to the LEFT, and you should be looking at the outside of

## The Southern Wall

Unfortunately the Model is not up to date and does not reflect the latest archaeological discoveries that have been made along this wall. So please refer to the diagram below.

**The Mikvot (Ritual Baths).** Everyone visiting the Temple Mount had to be made ritually pure, and for this purpose a series of large pools (No. 1 on diagram below) were located to the RIGHT of the Wide Stairway. These pools were enclosed in buildings, and people would undress and then immerse themselves in the water and be blessed by a priest. Therefore, I place the following events in this area.

It is the custom among Jews that on the eighth day after the birth every male child is dedicated. Luke 2:2:

> And when eight days were accomplished for the circumcising of the child, whose name was called Jesus.

THE SOUTHERN WALL

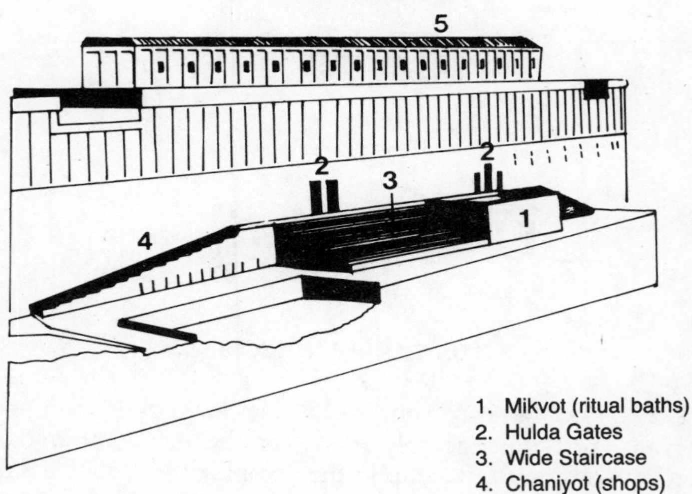


1. Mikvot (ritual baths)
2. Hulda Gates
3. Wide Staircase
4. Chaniyot (shops)
5. Royal Stoa

Another event that likely took place at the Mikvot was Peter's baptism of three thousand converts. (See page 169.)

**The Hulda Gates.** Set in the wall itself are two entrance gates (No. 2 on the diagram). The Model shows them both as double entrance gates. This is incorrect. The entrance gate, on the RIGHT, was a Triple Gate. The pilgrims would assemble on the Wide Stairway, take their ritual baths, and then enter upon the Mount through the Triple Hulda Gate, which led to an underground passage and from there exited on the Mount. After finishing their business on the Mount, they would exit through the underground passage leading to the Double Hulda Gate on the LEFT.

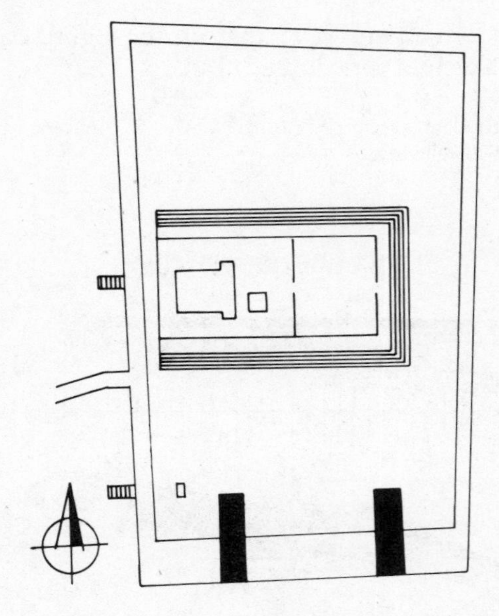

HULDA GATES ON THE MOUNT

**The Wide Stairway.** Since the Wide Stairway (No. 3 on the diagram) was the assembly point for the many thousands of pilgrims coming to worship in the Temple, it was a logical place for the priests and judges to address the crowds. This theory was borne out recently by the discovery of a stone plaque with the word *Zachinem* in Hebrew inscribed into its face. In English this means "Elders" which is what the members of the supreme court (Sanhedrin) of the time were called. Jesus, wanting to address as many people as possible at one time, may very well have preached to the pilgrims from the Wide Stairway. (See page 170.)

**The Pinnacle (or Highest Point of the Temple).** The last New Testament reference we are going to make here is at the far end of the Southern Wall at the corner. This is the Pinnacle of the Temple, where Satan tempted Jesus. (See page 171.)

For many years tradition has placed the Pinnacle on the southeast corner of the Mount. Recent finds indicate that it may have been the southwest corner that is referred to.

We are now going to move a little to the LEFT again and view the Hippodrome and the Theater.

MODEL OF THE HIPPODROME

## STOP 6: THE HIPPODROME

We learned of this structure from the historian Josephus. However, as of this writing, no archaeological remains of this building have been found. The presence of a sports arena so close to the Temple itself could have caused tension between the orthodox and Hellenized Jews. Another building that likewise may have caused dissension was the

## STOP 7: THEATER

To locate the theater move a little to the LEFT, and align yourself with the Theater as shown in the photograph below. Notice the small houses in front of the Hippodrome. Then there is an empty space and then a large building. Position yourself in front of the large building. Look past this building up the hill. The Theater is the building with a wide plaza, with stairs on either side and arched windows facing you.

As with the Hippodrome, no architectural evidence has been turned up in the city to locate this monumental building. However, a very interesting artifact has been found: a theater ticket. It

MODEL OF ROMAN THEATER

was carved out of bone and inscribed "Wing Seat No. 10," in Greek.

This Herodian theater had an open-air auditorium, formed by steps on which the audience sat in a semicircle. A back wall behind the stage acted as the amplifier for the actors' voices.

Now look at the palatial homes that surround the theater. That is today's Jewish Quarter. In Jesus' day it was named the Upper City. It lies on top of the hill, and its gracious homes enjoyed a cool breeze in summer and a magnificent view.

Notice the houses on the lower slope of the hill. This is where the poorer residents of Jerusalem lived.

Now move down the hill to your LEFT. The area enclosed by a double wall on the Model is the City of David. Near the bottom of the City of David is the Pool of Siloam. It is shown as a structure with a raised platform surrounded on all sides by columns.

## STOP 8: THE POOL OF SILOAM

We will not be visiting this site, since it is in an out-of-the-way place. But we might recall the New Testament events now. John 9:1 and 7:

> And as Jesus passed by, he saw a man which was blind from his birth.
>
> And said unto him, Go, wash in the pool of Siloam. . . . He went his way therefore, and washed, and came seeing.

Another event that took place near the Pool of Siloam was the collapse of a tower, killing eighteen men. Jesus used the incident as an example. Luke 13:4:

> Or those eighteen, upon whom the tower in Siloam fell, and slew them, think ye that they were sinners above all men, that dwelt in Jerusalem?

Now turn your attention to the area between the Model and the chain fence. It appears as a dirt track. Its actual location in the city is in the Valley of Hinnom. This area was known as

## STOP 9: ACELDAMA, THE FIELD OF BLOOD

Judas, after his betrayal of Jesus, suffered remorse and returned to the Temple, where he threw down the thirty pieces of silver he had received for the betrayal. Then he committed suicide. Since the money was blood money, the Temple officials did not put it back into the Treasury. What they did with it is told to us in Acts 1:18–19:

> Now this man purchased a field with the reward of iniquity; and falling headlong, he burst asunder in the midst, and all his bowels gushed out.
>
> And it was known unto all the dwellers of Jerusalem insomuch as that field is called in their proper tongue, Aceldama, that is to say, The field of blood.

Now continue up the hill. You are approaching

## STOP 10: MOUNT ZION

On Walk 3 you got a feeling of this elegant and sacred area. After we left the Cenacle, we walked down a very steep road to reach Saint Peter in Gallicantu Church, which is located at the lower part of Mount Zion.

In 1536, the Turkish sultan, Suleiman the Magnificent, rebuilt the city walls. For an unknown reason he did not include Mount Zion within them. In Jesus' day the priestly class lived on Mount Zion, as is indicated by the lovely expensive homes shown on the Model.

Now continue a little past the light post on the LEFT and then align yourself with

## STOP 11: DAVID'S TOMB

The tomb shown in the Model has no known relation to what King David's Tomb may actually have looked like. Mount Zion today can only be called the traditional site of David's Tomb. Our interest in this area lies in two specific events.

MODEL OF DAVID'S TOMB

## STOP 12: THE ROOM OF THE LAST SUPPER

This is the "large upper room" where Jesus and his disciples celebrated the Passover and the Last Supper and where, later, the disciples were visited by the Holy Spirit. Mark 14:15 and Acts 2:2 and 6:

> And he will show you a large upper room furnished and prepared: there make ready for us.
>
> And suddenly there came a sound from heaven, as of a rushing mighty wind, and it filled all the house where they were sitting.
>
> Now when this was noised abroad, the multitude came together, and were confounded, because everyman heard them speak in his own language.

## STOP 13: THE HOUSE OF CAIAPHAS

A little to the LEFT of where you are now standing is a large, spread-out, multicolumned building. This is one of the proposed sites for the house of High Priest Caiaphas. After Jesus was arrested in the Garden of Gethsemane he was taken to the high priest's house. We cannot be certain of the exact location. The Model places it in the Armenian Garden.

**MODEL OF THE LUXURIOUS HOME OF HIGH PRIEST CAIAPHAS**

As you recall, we visited another site on Mount Zion that may also be the actual house of Caiaphas. Unfortunately there is not enough evidence to say precisely which is the correct location for the house of the high priest.

We have two more stops here at the Model, and then you can take a rest over a cup of coffee at the snack bar and gift shop (closed on Saturdays and Jewish holidays), located up ahead and off to the LEFT.

First, let's walk toward the three large towers in the Model, up ahead. Just before the towers, stop and look into

## STOP 14: KING HEROD'S PALACE

It is agreed among historians and scholars that Herod the Great felt very threatened concerning his hold on his kingdom. The two main factors in this were the turbulent geopolitical situation, in which world powers used Judea as a pawn, and the plotting and scheming for power among Herod's immediate royal family and royal court. His insecurities are reflected in the way he built his palace. It looks more like a fort than a dwelling place, what with all the watchtowers and walls on all sides.

**MODEL OF KING HEROD'S PALACE**

From a New Testament point of view, our interest in this palace is that it has been proposed as an alternative site of the Judgment of Jesus.

Look into the Model and locate the towers of the Antonia Fortress. Between where you are standing and the Antonia is an outcropping of rock with some vegetation around it. There should be an entrance gate in the city wall to the right of the outcropping. This represents

## STOP 15: THE TRADITIONAL SITE OF CALVARY

We will visit this site on the last walk. It is where the Church of the Holy Sepulcher is located today. Notice that this location was indeed outside the city walls in the time of Jesus, which is strong evidence in its favor, as by law all Jewish burials took place outside the city walls. We will also visit the other proposed site of Calvary, the Garden Tomb.

I hope that you are now well prepared for the last two walks, which take place within what were the city limits in Jesus' time.

Before you start, I strongly urge that you reread the section "The Temple and the Temple Mount" in the Introduction (pages 19–35). It deals with the rules and regulations of the Second Temple during Jesus' day and is intended to give you an accurate feeling of the times.

## ROUTE OF WALK 5

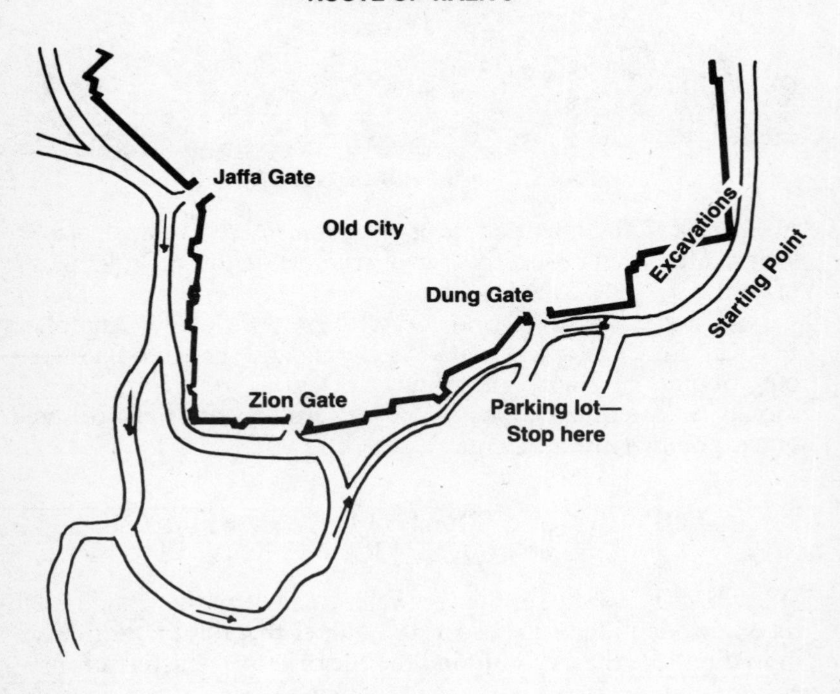

WALK

# 5

# *The Temple Mount*

| EVENT | SITE |
|---|---|
| | The Southern Wall Excavations |
| • Pilgrims' gathering place | Southern Wall excavations |
| • Jesus addresses the crowds | The Wide Stairway |
| • Pentecost | Ritual Baths *(Mikvot)* |
| • Entering the Temple Mount | Hulda Gates |
| • The Temptation | The Pinnacle |
| • Destruction of Jerusalem | Excavations at southwest corner |
| | The Temple Mount |
| • Pilgrims' entrance/exit | The Hulda Gates |
| • Jesus is questioned | The Royal Stoa |
| • He overturns the tables | The Royal Stoa |
| • Peter and the beggar | The Beautiful Gate |
| • Paul's arrest | The Antonia Fortress |
| | The Antonia Fortress |
| • The Judgment | Ecce Homo |
| • Game of the King | Antonia Fortress |

Today's tour goal is to acquaint ourselves with the areas in and around the Temple Mount associated with various events in Jesus' life and with incidents involving Peter and Paul. We will also review Jesus' examination and condemnation by Pilate.

## SPECIAL SUGGESTIONS

**Proper dress.** You will not be allowed entrance onto the Temple Mount if you are wearing shorts, and women must have blouses that cover their arms to the elbows.

**Visiting hours.** The Temple Mount is open to non-Muslim visitors Saturday through Thursday. The hours are 8 A.M. to 11:30 P.M. and 1 P.M. to 3 P.M. Friday, the Muslim sabbath, only Muslims are allowed on the Mount. Visiting hours to this site change often, so it is best to check the day before.

**The Sisters of Sion.** Open in winter October 1 to March 31, 8:30 A.M. to 4 P.M., in summer April 1 to September 30, 8:30 A.M. to 12:30 P.M. and 2:30 to 5:30 P.M. Closed Sunday.

## GETTING TO THE STARTING POINT

The starting point for this walk is the Southern Wall excavations.

**By Bus from West Jerusalem.** Take the Egged city bus No. 1, which you can pick up at the Central Bus Station on Jaffa Road. The last stop is outside the Dung Gate. Cross the street and follow the city walls down the hill until you reach the excavation site at the bottom of the hill.*Align yourself with the broad staircase made of white stone. It is located somewhat to the* RIGHT *of the slate-gray dome of El Aqsa Mosque.*

**By Bus from East Jerusalem.** From the Central Bus Station in East Jerusalem (near the Damascus Gate) take bus No. 76. It will be circling the city walls, and in about ten minutes you will pass a very large open excavation site on your RIGHT. Signal the driver to let you off opposite these excavations. (You know that you have gone too far if you see the sign reading "Pool of Siloam.") See italicized passage above for where to stand at the excavation site.

**By Foot (to the Dung Gate).** Enter the Old City through the Jaffa Gate and bear RIGHT once inside the city. You will be walking on the Armenian Patriarchate Road. Follow this road all the way to the end, about a fifteen-minute walk. When you reach the Dung Gate, follow the directions for West Jerusalem.

**By Car.** Drive past the Jaffa Gate. At the bottom of the hill STOP. We are going to turn LEFT, but be very careful, for there is fast-moving traffic here. After your LEFT turn, continue along until you pass the Dung Gate (you will see the sign) and at the bottom of the hill past the gate is a parking lot on the RIGHT. Park here. The excavations are across the road. See the italicized passage for where to stand.

## Some Very Probable Sites

Today's walk is completely different from all of the previous walks. The past walks have taken us to shrines that are dedicated to some of the *possible* sites that commemorate Jesus' last week in Jerusalem. Today we are going to be visiting some very probable sites.

These sites are directly connected with Jesus' last days. We can actually walk today in areas that the science of archaeology tells us were New Testament sites.

THE DOME OF THE ROCK SUPERIMPOSED ON THE SITE OF THE TEMPLE

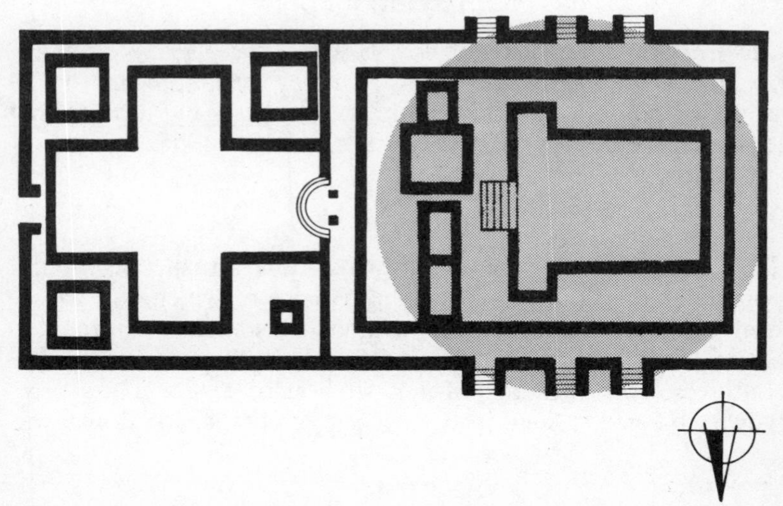

Let's begin by familiarizing ourselves with the excavation site.

## THE SOUTHERN WALL EXCAVATIONS

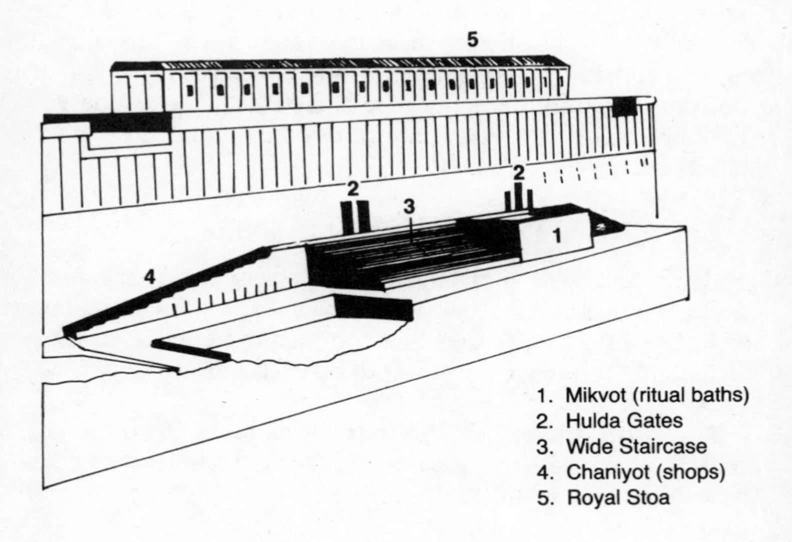


### The Assembly Point

The area you are looking at now is where the pilgrims from all over the world assembled. In this area they would prepare themselves for going up on the Mount to offer their sacrifices. Now let's learn about how this site functioned in Jesus' day.

### The Royal Stoa

The Royal Stoa (No. 5 on drawing) was actually the upper portion of the Southern Wall, the remains of which you see in front of you. It was a two-story colonnaded structure that ran the entire length of the Southern Wall. Its entrance was at the southwest corner of the Mount. It housed a series of shops, which changed money into currency acceptable for donations and where pilgrims could purchase animals for sacrificing. It was almost completely destroyed by the Romans in A.D. 70. As to its beauty, Josephus, who was widely traveled and had visited imperial Rome, said in his *Antiquities of the Jews,* 15:430:

> And this portico was more deserving of mention than any under the sun.

## The Mikvot (Ritual Baths)

To the RIGHT of the Wide Staircase in front of you was a large complex of buildings (No. 1 on drawing) containing many pools that had been cut into the bedrock. Jewish law required that each person who wished to enter the Temple area had to be ritually pure, and this purification was carried out by immersion in the pool under the watchful eye of a priest. So we can envision Jesus and his followers immersing themselves in these very same baths before they entered the Temple Mount.

Mary too underwent purification, after Jesus' birth. Luke 2:22:

> And when the days of her purification, according to the law of Moses, were accomplished, they brought him to Jerusalem, to present him to the Lord.

Another event that we locate here is Peter's baptism of three thousand converts. Acts 2:41:

> And they that gladly received his word were baptized: and the same day there were added unto them about three thousand souls.

## The Wide Staircase

Most archaeologists agree that these stairs (No. 3 on drawing) are the major find of this excavation. This is the same staircase that was here when Jesus walked around this area.

After their purification the pilgrims would climb this staircase to enter the Mount. The staircase is 215 feet wide and contains 30 steps, alternating wide steps and narrow steps. They were cut into the natural base rock of the Mount. The rabbis moved their offices to the top of the stairs, since it was the ideal place to speak to thousands of people at one time. It is logical to assume that Jesus may have used this same ideal location to preach to the crowds. Matthew 23:1, 9, 11, 17, and 24:

> Then spake Jesus to the multitude and his disciples.
>
> And call no man your Father upon this earth: for one is your Father, which is in Heaven.
>
> But he that is greatest among you shall be your servant.
>
> Ye fools, and blind: for whether is greater, the gold, or the temple that sanctifieth the gold?
>
> Ye blind guides! which strain at a gnat, and swallow a camel.

For me possibly the most exciting moment in the writing of this book was when I stood on the Wide Staircase, looked out to my LEFT at the graves (white-stone sepulchers) on the Mount of Olives, and read Matthew 23:27:

> Woe unto you, scribes and Pharisees, hypocrites! for ye are like unto whited sepulchres [white tombstones], which indeed appear beautiful outward, but are within full of dead men's bones, and of all uncleanness.

Could Jesus have stood here and pointed to the tombs as he spoke?

## The Triple Hulda Gates

The Triple Gates (No. 2 on drawing) may be a bit difficult to locate at first since they were blocked in by the Crusaders. They are located to the RIGHT of the Wide Staircase and are set in the wall itself. This gate served as the main entrance onto the Temple Mount for the pilgrims. Mishnah Middot 1.2:

> All who entered the Temple Mount entered by the right [Triple] Hulda Gate and went round and went out left [Double Hulda Gate]. The only exception was in the case of mourners and those who had been excommunicated.

## The Double Hulda Gate

The remains of this gate (No. 2 on the drawing) are even more difficult to locate. Look at the slate gray dome. Let your eyes travel down and to the LEFT. A wall was built right into the Double Gate, and as a result we can only see the corner decorative stone. This served as the exit for most pilgrims.

Now we will be going up on the Temple Mount itself. But since the Hulda Gates are blocked off, we will have to turn LEFT, walk up the hill, and enter the city through the Dung Gate. It is the first gate you will reach on your RIGHT.

Walk inside the Dung Gate and prepare to open the bags or packages you are carrying for the security officer up ahead. After passing the security booth, stop about fifteen paces ahead next to the chain-link fence. On the RIGHT is

## THE SOUTHWEST CORNER OF THE TEMPLE MOUNT

Looking at the corner, try to visualize it as being twice as high in Jesus' day.

### The Pinnacle

At the very top of the corner of the walls was the Pinnacle—that is, the highest level of the Temple Mount. This Pinnacle is where Satan tempts Jesus.

We first meet Satan at Mount Qarental near Jericho. Matthew 4:3, 4:

> And when the tempter [Satan] came to him, he said, If thou be the Son of God, command that these stones be made bread
>
> But he answered and said, It is written, Man shall not live by bread alone, but by every word that proceedeth out of the mouth of God.

We next meet him in the Holy City. Matthew 4:5–7:

> Then the devil taketh him up into the holy city, and setteth him on a pinnacle of the temple,
>
> And saith unto him, If thou be the Son of God cast thyself down. . . .
>
> Jesus said unto him, It is written again, Thou shalt not tempt the Lord thy God.

Now let's locate Robinson's Arch. Starting from the corner of the wall go LEFT. About halfway up the wall and under the four

THE REMAINS OF ROBINSON'S ARCH

windows, you will see stones jutting out of the wall. These are the only remains of what we call today

## Robinson's Arch

This monumental arched stairway was named after Edward Robinson, the archaeologist who discovered it in 1883. This massive stairway, leading up to the Royal Stoa of the Temple Mount, was used principally by the priests and the pilgrims.

Look down below you, at the area between the wall and the wooden walkway. Using the drawing below, locate

## The Shops

These particular shops (No. 4 on drawing) were located under the staircase of Robinson's arch. They sold souvenirs for the pilgrims to purchase. In effect this area could be called the shopping mall of Jerusalem in the time of Jesus. In this shop area, archaeologists found coins from all over the Roman empire.

Now it's time to walk up onto the Temple Mount itself. Bear RIGHT, and walk up the ramp. Take about twenty-five steps, then stop and look down into the excavations on your LEFT.

## THREE HUGE HERODIAN STONES

Those three huge stones, each weighing about eighty tons, were once sitting up on top of the wall. They were thrown down by the Romans when they destroyed the city in A.D. 70. They are thus living evidence of the grim thoroughness of the Destruction. Cross over to the other side and look down at the view of the Western Wall.

## THE WESTERN WALL

The Western Wall is a historical, religious, and national monument and has been the focus of Jewish attention for centuries. There are several reasons for this.

DEVOUT JEWS PRAYING AT THE WESTERN WALL

This retaining wall of the Temple Mount, which existed in Jesus' day, is the only surviving remnant of the Temple, and as such, it is a memorial to Israel's days of religious and national glory. The Wall is also a symbol of the Jewish people, who, like it, have managed to survive for thousands of years, in spite of the many efforts to destroy them.

Still others relate to the Wall as the holiest place in Judaism and as a temporary substitute for the Temple. Thus for a multitude of reasons the Western Wall, also known as the Wailing Wall, is one of the cornerstones of Jewish existence and that of the State of Israel as well.

It is customary for visitors to the Wall to write down their innermost prayers on pieces of paper and place them in cracks in the wall. I suggest that you pay a visit to the Wall during your stay in Jerusalem.

Since this is a holy site, modest dress is required—for women, no slacks or shorts, sleeves to the elbow; for men no shorts or tank tops. Men are required to have their heads covered. Disposable hats are available free of charge at the entrance to the men's section.

Continue up the ramp, and prepare to open your purses and packages for a second security check. The Mount is open 8 to 11:30 A.M. and 1 to 2 P.M. Closed Friday and Muslim Holidays.

Even though all of the buildings that Jesus saw on this Mount are gone, the Mount is the same size as it was in Jesus' day. If you visited the Model of Jerusalem in A.D. 66, you have in your mind's eye how the buildings did appear to Jesus. We have many New Testament events to recall up here, so please refer to the diagram on the opposite page.

## THE TEMPLE MOUNT

After familiarizing yourself with the drawing of the Temple Mount (opposite), walk straight ahead to the ticket booth and buy a ticket, which allows you to visit both El Aqsa Mosque and the Dome of the Rock. Once you have your ticket, continue walking in the direction you were headed, passing the large mosque with the slate-gray dome on the RIGHT. Stop when you reach a set of stairs leading down to below the Mount. You can recognize the stairs by the green metal fence surrounding them on three sides. This is the exit to the Double Hulda Gate.

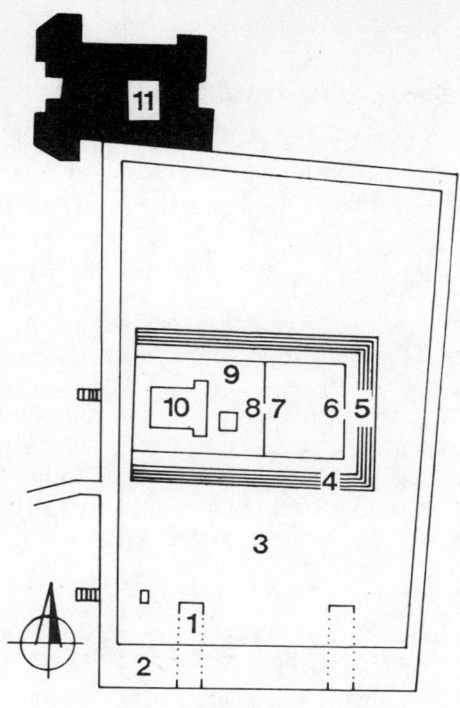


| No. | Today's Site | *In Jesus' Day* |
|---|---|---|
| 1. | Hulda Gate Exit | Hulda Gate Exit |
| 2. | El Aqsa Mosque | The Royal Stoa |
| 3. | Open Courtyard | Court of the Gentiles |
| 4. | Stone Wall | Balustrade |
| 5. | Five Arches | Beautiful Gate |
| 6. | Upper Plaza | Court of the Women |
| 7. | Dome of the Chain | Nicanor Gates |
| 8. | Dome of the Chain | Court of the Israelites |
| 9. | Dome of the Rock | Court of the Priests |
| 10. | Dome of the Rock | Temple—Holy of Holies |
| 11. | Muslim Boy's School | The Antonia Fortress |

## The Double Hulda Gate

As I mentioned before, this (No. 1 on drawing) was the exit the pilgrims took from the Mount. It led them through an underground passage, to the Hulda Gate. Standing where you are, to your right is the silver-gray dome of the El Aqsa Mosque. In Jesus' time the mosque, of course, didn't exist. In its place was

## The Royal Stoa

The Stoa (No. 2 on drawing) was 900 feet in length and 137 in height. It ran along the entire length of the Southern Wall. Let's now review some of the events that may have taken place in and around this site.

In an attempt to discredit Jesus with the Romans as well as the Zealots, a group of people asked him a trick question. Among the many grievances of the Jews was that they were required to pay a heavy poll tax to Tiberius Caesar, the Roman emperor. This was one of the main political issues of the day. Anyone speaking against the tax was considered a rebel by the Romans and subject to imprisonment; anyone supporting it was considered a traitor by the Zealots. Several men approached Jesus and put a question to him that, they thought, could not be answered without getting him into trouble with one group or the other. Mark 12:14–17:

> Is it lawful to give tribute to Caesar or not?
>
> Shall we give or shall we not give? But he, knowing their hypocrisy, said unto them, Why tempt ye me? Bring me a penny that I may see it.
>
> And they brought it. And he saith unto them, Whose is this image and superscription? And they said unto him, Caesar's.
>
> And Jesus, answering, said unto them, Render to Caesar the things that are Caesar's, and to God the things that are God's. And they marvelled at him.

## The Shops in the Royal Stoa

Many shops to service the pilgrims were located here. They stocked merchandise that was mainly used for the sacrifices every pilgrim made through the priests. In addition to the sacrifices, everyone was required to pay a sheckel or half-sheckel to the Temple Treasury to help support this tremendous operation. However, coins that bore a human or animal image were not accepted by the Treasury because of the prohibition of the Second Commandment. Exodus 20:4:

> Thou shalt not make unto thee any graven image, or any likeness of any thing that is in heaven above, or that is in the earth beneath, or that is in the water under the earth.

Since the pilgrims came from all over the Roman world, they arrived with pagan coins, and these had to be exchanged for Jewish coins, which were imprinted with floral or geometrical designs. Therefore money changers were required near the Mount.

It seems that commerce being conducted to close to the Temple itself angered Jesus. Matthew 21:12:

> And Jesus went into the temple of God, and cast out all them that sold and bought in the temple, and overthrew the tables of the moneychangers, and the seats of them that sold doves.

Now, standing where you are, turn around and face the Golden Dome of the Rock.

## The Court of the Gentiles

Everyone entering the Mount from the Triple Hulda Gate would exit onto the Court of the Gentiles (No. 3 on drawing). It was the largest court on the Mount, being the outermost one. Jews would proceed from this court to the inner courts closer and leading to the Temple. Non-Jews were restricted to this court only. Just as today many visitors to Jerusalem come on the Mount to visit the Dome of the Rock, so the Temple was a major tourist attraction to all visitors to Jerusalem.

Looking ahead, notice the low stone wall with a line of pine trees above it. This could have been the approximate location of a screened wall that separated the Court of the Gentiles from the inner courts of the Temple. This was called

## The Balustrade

All along this wall (No. 4 on drawing) signs warned non-Jews not to pass this wall, on pain of immediate death.

A fragment of warning notice in Greek and Latin was found on the Mount. Translation of the entire notice:

> No foreigner is to enter within the balustrade and enclosure around the Temple area. Whoever is caught will have himself to blame for his death, which will follow.

Now walk back toward the large building with the slate-gray dome that you passed a few minutes ago. This is

## El Aqsa Mosque

El Aqsa is a place of public prayer for Muslims. This mosque in Jerusalem is considered the third holiest site in Islam, after Mecca and Medina in Saudia Arabia.

The mosque, which was built in A.D. 710, is 190 feet wide, 270 feet long and holds up to 5,000 worshippers at one time. It has seven aisles, and 114 stained glass windows, and its dome is lead covered.

In A.D. 746, an earthquake destroyed the mosque. Because there was no money to pay for rebuilding it, the authorities ordered the massive doors, which were inlaid with gold and silver, to be melted down and minted into coins,which were used to pay for its reconstruction.

THE DOME OF THE ROCK

In A.D. 1099, during the Crusader occupation of Jerusalem, El Aqsa was converted into both a palace for visiting Crusader kings and a church. In July 1951, the grandfather of King Hussein of Jordan, King Abdullah, was assassinated outside the mosque by Arab extremists. In 1969, a magnificent pulpit *(Minbar)* was destroyed by a fire started by a demented Australian, Dennis Michael Rohan.

Before entering, you must remove your shoes. Leave them outside in front of the building. To save yourself time and frustration, make a mental note of where you are leaving them.

As you enter, notice that seating is not provided for the worshippers. Since Muslims kneel during prayer, instead of chairs and benches, the floor is covered with prayer rugs. As you walk toward the front of the mosque, notice the various ways in which the ceiling has been finished. It varies from wood planking to plaster to painting to precast masonry tiles.

When you reach the front of the mosque, locate the double row of columns. These columns are a test for the faithful. In order to determine if someone is worthy of entering heaven, he must first pass between the row of columns without touching them.

When you have completed your visit to El Aqsa, leave through the same door you entered. After retrieving your shoes, walk straight ahead and stop at the large water fountain that is enclosed by a blue metal fence. This is

## El Kas Fountain

El Kas means cup, and this fountain got its name from the goblet-shaped bowl you see in front of you. The cistern that supplies it with fresh water is the largest on the Mount, with a capacity of 2 million gallons.

The spigots above the stone seats, which encircle the fountain, are for the faithful to wash their hands, faces, and feet, which is required of all Muslims before entering a mosque.

We are now going up on the raised platform that contains the Golden Dome of the Rock. Walk up the wide staircase in front of you. As you approach the four arches, notice that there is a

EL KAS FOUNTAIN

sundial with Arabic numbers. Once on top, turn RIGHT and walk across the Mount toward the five arches to the right. If, when you are standing under the five arches, you are looking at the golden onion domes of the Russian Church, you are in the right place.

## The Beautiful Gate

You will recall that, as Peter was passing through this gate area (No. 5 on drawing), a beggar asked him for alms. Acts 3:6 and 8:

> Then Peter said, Silver and gold have I none: but such as I have give I thee: In the name of Jesus Christ of Nazareth, rise up and walk.
>
> And he, leaping up, stood, and walked, and entered with them into the temple, walking, and leaping, and praising God.

Now walk forward thirty steps. You are now standing in what then was called

## The Court of the Women

This court (No. 6 on drawing) was as close as women were permitted to enter—with the exception of Sukkoth (Feast of Tabernacles), when they were allowed to bring their sacrifices directly to the Court of the Priests.

The Court of the Women was also the Treasury. Located here were collection boxes. This is probably why the beggar chose to sit in front of the entrance gate to this court. Let's now recall Mark 12:41–43:

> And Jesus sat over against the treasury, and beheld how the people cast money into the treasury: and many that were rich cast in much.
>
> And there came a certain poor widow, and she threw in two mites, which make a farthing.
>
> And he called unto him his disciples, and saith unto them, Verily I say to you, That this poor widow hath cast more in, than all they which have cast into the treasury.

This court was also apparently the scene of Judas' attempt to return the thirty pieces of silver. (See page 120.)

Continue ahead toward the black-domed building that seems to be a model of the Dome of the Rock (it's called the Dome of the Chain), and stop in front of it. Let's now go back two thousand years. Imagine yourself approaching

## The Nicanor Gates

As you approach the gates (No. 7 on drawing), the priests are lined up all along the circular stairway, some playing their beautiful musical instruments, and others singing and chanting Psalms.

Today because of the Dome of the Chain, we cannot proceed directly ahead, but that is where the next inner court of the Temple was. It was called

## The Court of the Israelites

There were three strata of Jews at that time, which had been determined by the twelve tribes. They were ranked according to their status: the priestly class *(Kohanim),* the Levites, and the ordinary people called Israelites. Only male Israelites were allowed to pass to this court (No. 8 on drawing) from the Nicanor Gates. They presented their sacrifices to the priests, who were in the next inner area, the Court of the Priests.

## The Court of the Priests

This court (No. 9 on drawing) was restricted to the priestly class. It was their responsibility to receive the sacrifices from the people and bestow their blessing. All of these courts led up to

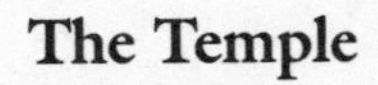

## The Temple

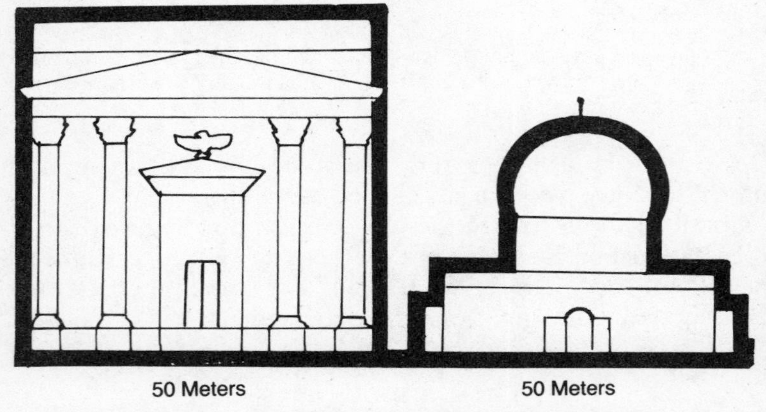


**THE TEMPLE AS COMPARED TO THE DOME OF THE ROCK**

Most archaeologists believe that the Temple (No. 9 on drawing) stood where the Dome of the Rock stands today. The sanctuary, which contained the Holy of Holies, stood about 200 feet tall, according to Josephus. Given the massive size of the entire complex, one can imagine that not many people took Jesus too seriously when he predicted its total destruction. Matthew 24:2:

> And Jesus said unto them, See ye not all these things? Verily I say unto you, There shall not be left here one stone upon another, that shall not be thrown down.

Although I hate to break into the theme of the walk at this point, I don't see how anyone can visit the Temple Mount without visiting the Dome of the Rock, which is considered by many people to be one of the most beautiful buildings in the world. The entrance is on the opposite side of the Mount.

## The Dome of the Rock
## (Qubbet el-Sakhra)

The Dome of the Rock was built by Abdel Malek, a Muslim ruler of Jerusalem in 691 A.D., in order to divert to Jerusalem some of the lucrative pilgrimage traffic that was going to Mecca in Saudi Arabia. The architecture of this building indicates that it was copied from the basic design of the Church of the Holy Sepulcher,which at the time was the outstanding building in Jerusalem. Both these buildings have an octagonal shape within a circle, which expresses an ancient concept that Jerusalem is the center of the earth.

The Dome is supported by twelve round marble pillars. The sixteen windows of the cupola are of stained glass on a gold background. When the sunlight shines through them, it throws an extraordinary light on the bedrock below, over which this shrine was built.

An amusing story connected with this site is that a later Muslim ruler named al-Mawan decided that he would like to be remembered as the builder of the Dome of the Rock. His plan was simple. He ordered his stonemasons to remove Abdel

Malek's name from the dedication plaque and to insert his name in its place. However, he forgot to tell them to change the date. As the plaque reads today, al-Mawan dedicated the Dome of the Rock two hundred years before he was born.

The magnificent blue glazed tiles running around the drum serve more than just a decorative purpose. They tell the story in Kufic script of the Prophet Mohammed's Night Journey. Mohammed, the founder of Islam, dreamed that he ascended to the Seven Heavens on his mystical flying horse, el-Baraq, accompanied by the Archangel Gabriel.

The bedrock over which this shrine was built has two depressions in the face of the rock. Muslims believe they were made by Mohammed's horse when he ascended.

Before entering, remove your shoes and again remember where you are leaving them. Once inside, walk straight ahead and look up at the interior of the dome, which is the outstanding feature of this building. The Arabesque design is of plaster gilded with 22 karat gold. This outstanding work indicates the level of art reached during the heyday of Jerusalem's Arab rulers.

When you reach the railing surrounding the Rock, notice the stone frieze. These miniature columns from the time of the Crusaders were carved by hand from a single rock.

Now walk around the Rock going to your RIGHT. Many scholars suggest this may be the rock that King David bought from the Jebusites for a threshing floor. It is not uncommon in the Holy Land for one religion to build its shrines over the sites used earlier by others.

Stop when you reach the large box suspended over the Rock. Muslims believe that it contains strands of Mohammed's beard and that below the box is an imprint of the sole of his foot when he ascended to the Seven Heavens. Visitors are allowed to place their hands inside the bottom of the box to feel the depressions in the Rock.

Continue along in the same direction you were headed, and when you reach the stairway on your LEFT, go down into the cave, which is located directly below the sacred Rock. This cave is called the Pit of the Souls, and the faithful believe that the spirits of the dead meet here twice a week. The hollow sound you hear when you stamp your feet has given this place a second name, the Well of the Spirits. As you head back upstairs, notice the stone carved miniature pillars to the right of the first step.

Once back upstairs, going toward the exit, take your time and notice the outstanding Corinthian capitals, the magnificent windows, and the decorated ceiling.

When you leave the Dome of the Rock, retrieve your shoes and go back down to the lower platform, heading in the direction of the tall minaret in the northwest corner.

Below, you will see the Al-Omariya Muslim Boys' School. In Jesus' day here stood

## The Antonia Fortress

**AL-OMARIYA BOYS' SCHOOL, ON THE SITE OF THE ANTONIA.**

The Antonia (No. 11 on the drawing on page 175) was a very tall fortress and completely dominated the Mount. To judge its height, you can figure that it was about one and a half times as tall as the minaret next to the school. The Antonia Fortress is the ideal place to recall Paul's arrest and defense.

The Antonia is where the Romans took Paul to protect him from the angry crowd. He had been accused of bringing non-Jews past the Balustrade and into an inner courts of the Temple. As I mentioned before, a violation of that rule was punishable by immediate death by stoning. Acts 21:28 and 31:

> Crying out, Men of Israel, help: this is the man that teacheth all men every where against the people and the law, and this place: and further, brought Greeks also into the Temple, and hath polluted this holy place.
>
> And as they went about to kill him, tidings came unto the chief captain of the band [Romans], that all Jerusalem was in an uproar.

To quell the disturbance the Roman captain ordered Paul to be taken up the steps and into the Antonia Fortress for further questioning. Acts 21:37:

> And as Paul was to be led to the castle [Antonia], he said unto the chief captain, May I speak unto thee? Who said, Canst thou speak Greek?

The captain was obviously taken aback when Paul spoke to him in Greek. He had incorrectly assumed that the prisoner was a false prophet from Egypt who had caused much disturbance with his followers in Jerusalem a short time before. Paul identified himself as a Jew of Tarsus, a city in Cilicia (today part of Turkey). Then he asked for permission to address the crowd.

He spoke to them in Hebrew, telling them that he was born in Tarsus and grew up in Jerusalem, where he studied Jewish law under the great sage Rabbi Gamaliel. He was known then as Saul. He had been instrumental, he said, in seeking out and exposing the followers of Jesus. He was on his way to Damascus to root out some more of Jesus' followers when the following occurred. Acts 22:6–8:

> And it came to pass, that, as I made my journey, and was come nigh unto Damascus about noon, suddenly there shone from heaven a great light round about me.
>
> And I fell unto the ground, and heard a voice saying unto me, Saul, Saul, why persecutest thou me?
>
> And I answered, Who art thou, Lord? And he said unto me, I am Jesus of Nazareth, whom thou persecutest.

Those who were accompanying Paul on the journey to Damascus were unaware of this vision taking place. Paul was temporarily blinded from the glory of the light shining on him. His sight was restored by a man named Ananias, who then said, Acts 22:15:

> For thou shalt be his witness unto all men of what thou hast seen and heard.

After being baptized by Ananias, Paul returned to Jerusalem, where he was rejected by the authorities for his new beliefs.

We now learn of Paul's mission to preach the Gospels. Acts 22:21:

> And he [Jesus] said unto me, Depart: for I will send thee far hence unto the Gentiles.

The crowd, hearing the word "Gentile," was reminded once again that Paul was rumored to have violated the rules about bringing non-Jews into the inner courts, and began again to call for his immediate death. As the Roman soldiers were leading Paul into the Antonia Fortress to be scourged, Paul turned to a centurion and asked, Acts 22:25–26:

> Is it lawful for you to scourge a man that is a Roman, and uncondemned?

When the centurion heard that, he went and told the chief captain, saying,

> Take heed what thou doest: for this man is a Roman.

That is, Paul was a Roman citizen, a status he inherited from his father, who had been granted it probably for services to the Roman government. As a *civis Romanus,* no Roman would punish him unless he had been convicted by a Roman judge. Paul was also a Jew by birth and training, however, so the captain turned him over to the Sanhedrin.

The Sanhedrin, the supreme council and tribunal of the Jews, was composed of two political parties, the Pharisees, who believed in life after death, and the Sadducees, who did not. Paul addressed them. Acts 23:6:

> Men and brethren, I am a Pharisee, the son of a Pharisee: of the hope and resurrection of the dead I am called in question.

This caused quite a stir among the crowd, and those belonging to the Pharisee party declared that they found no evil in Paul, and that made the dispute worse.

Fearing more disturbances, the Roman captain ordered Paul to be rescued from the Sanhedrin and taken inside the Antonia for safekeeping, and decided that as a Roman citizen, Paul must be sent for trial to Roman authorities. He was taken to Caesarea and from there shipped to Rome.

While Paul was in Antonia, waiting to hear his fate, he had another visitation from Jesus. Acts 23:11:

> And the night following, the Lord stood by him and said, Be of good cheer, Paul: for as thou hast testified of me in Jerusalem, so must thou bear witness also at Rome.

Now for the last stop on today's tour. We are going to walk to the Convent of the Sisters of Sion, which is built within the remains of the Antonia Fortress. The Sisters of Sion— "Sion" being the French for Zion—are open in winter, October 1 to March 31, 8:30 A.M. to 4 P.M.; in summer, April 1 to September 30, 8:30 A.M. to 12:30 P.M., and 2:30 to 5:30 P.M. Closed Sunday.

Facing the minaret, go out the gate on the LEFT. Follow the street you are on until you reach the cross street; the sign reads "Via Dolorosa." Turn LEFT, and a few steps down the street you will be standing under

## THE ECCE HOMO ARCH

This arch, all that remains of the original Triple Arch, must be studied from two perspectives—that of tradition and that of scientific evidence.

**Tradition.** Many people believe that this arch marks the spot where the Roman Governor Pontius Pilate brought Jesus forth and presented him to the people wearing the crown of thorns and the purple robe and said, *"Ecce Homo"* ("Behold the man").

ECCE HOMO ARCH

**Scientific evidence.** Many archaeologists—and several sisters of Sion as well—agree that the arch under which you are standing is really from a later period and did not exist in Jesus' time. The evidence indicates that the Triple Arch of which we see one arch was built in A.D. 136 by the Roman Emperor Hadrian, after his victory over the Jews during the Bar Kokhba revolt.

However, I believe that it's important to have a place to commemorate this historic event, even if there is some question as to its authenticity.

## THE REMAINS OF THE ANTONIA FORTRESS

Our main interest on this site is with the Judgment of Jesus by Pilate and Jesus' treatment by his Roman guards, while he awaited his sentence of death by crucifixion. In addition to this site's being a place to recall the judgment, it is also an archaeological treat. Recent excavations have unearthed remains from Second Temple and Byzantine periods.

The most comprehensive tour of this site is given by the Sisters. Check with the office when the next tour is leaving. If you're continuing by yourself, once inside, turn RIGHT into the lecture hall, and stop at one of the models of the Antonia Fortress.

## The Model of the Antonia Fortress

As is clearly indicated in the model, the Antonia was comprised of four towers and an open courtyard. It dominated the Temple Mount as you can see in the photograph. The Roman garrison was stationed in the Antonia. Their job was to quell any insurrection that occurred on the Temple Mount.

**MODEL OF ROMAN HEADQUARTERS IN JERUSALEM**

After familiarizing yourself with the model, find a seat and let's recall the Judgment of Jesus.

There are two proposed sites of the Judgment. One is right here in the Antonia Fortress and the other is located near the Jaffa Gate, where the Palace of King Herod the Great once stood. There is some evidence for both sites, but no absolute proof for either. The New Testament states that Pilate was at "the palace,"

**MODEL OF THE TEMPLE AND THE ANTONIA FORTRESS**

but doesn't specify which one. So let's deal with the event rather than with the site.

Under the existing Jewish law of the day, the Sanhedrin did not have the legal right to impose the death penalty. This was reserved for the Romans. Therefore Jesus was brought before Pontius Pilate, Roman procurator of Judea, a kind of imperial steward. Jesus was charged with being disloyal to the Roman Emperor. Luke 23: 1 and 3:

> And the whole multitude of them arose and led him unto Pilate.
>
> And Pilate asked him, saying, Art thou the King of the Jews? And he answered him and said, Thou sayest it.

Pilate then declared that he found no fault with him, and upon learning that Jesus was from the Galilee area, he sent him to the man who was in charge of that area. He was the son of King Herod the Great, and his name was Herod Antipas. (This is the Herod who, at the request of his stepdaughter Salome, had John the Baptist beheaded.) He was visiting Jerusalem for the Passover holidays. When he questioned Jesus, Jesus refused to answer any of his questions, so Herod sent him back to Pilate.

We learn from the New Testament and other sources that it was customary, at the Passover season, for the Roman governor to grant amnesty (a full pardon) to one of the prisoners held by the government. Matthew 27:15 and 17:

> Now at that feast [Passover] the governor was wont to release unto the people a prisoner, whom they would. . . .
>
> Therefore when they were gathered together, Pilate said unto them, Whom will ye that I release unto you? Barabbas, or Jesus which is called Christ?

Barabbas was a prisoner then under sentence of death for insurrection and murder.

As Pilate sat down on the judgment seat, he was handed a note from his wife. It said that she had had a very disturbing dream concerning Jesus and that Pilate should not become involved in his case. But the hearing went on. Matthew 27:21:

> The governor answered and said unto them [the priests and elders], Whether of the twain will ye that I release unto you? They said, Barabbas.

Pilate demanded to know what evil Jesus had committed, but the crowd clamored loudly for Barabbas, so he gave in, called for a bowl of water, and publicly washed his hands (a symbolic act of disavowal), declaring that he was innocent of Jesus' blood. Luke 23:24:

> And Pilate gave sentence that it should be as they required.

After his sentence was passed, Jesus was turned over to the Roman guards to await his time of execution.

Let's now move along to a place called the Lithostrotos, and study some interesting evidence concerning Jesus' detention by the Romans before he was led to his Crucifixion.

On our way to the Lithostrotos, we will stop at the Struthion Pools. Walk to the end of the lecture hall and go down the staircase. When you reach the bottom, make an immediate SHARP RIGHT and head for the entrance in the corner. The light switch is on the wall next to the opening. As you enter the Struthion Pools, be careful not to hit your head on the low ceiling. Once inside, walk out to the end of the ramp that extends over the pools.

## THE STRUTHION POOLS

These pools existed in Jesus' day, and though this site is not directly connected with a New Testament event, you should see the pools as long as you are here.

These huge pools served as the water supply for the Antonia Fortress. To give you an indication of how large they are, imagine the modern wall in the rear taken away. Do you see the arches at the bottom of the left wall? On the other side is a pool the identical size of the one you are looking at.

Our next stop is the Lithostrotos (paved courtyard), and to get there, turn around and follow the walkway through the underground passage, which will lead you in a few minutes to an area enclosed by black metal chains. This is the Lithostrotos.

## THE LITHOSTROTOS

The word "Lithostrotos" is Greek and means "paved with stone," or "paved area"—a courtyard. Let's examine the evidence that this area was originally an open courtyard.

### The Drainage Channels

Locate the drainage channels cut into the floor. See the drawing to help you identify them. Now, what purpose can drainage channels serve in a room that has a roof? The answer is that the floor is ancient, and the ceiling that you see today is modern. This indicates that in Roman times this area was an open courtyard. Now walk ahead a few paces and look down at the paving stones inside the black-chained fence.

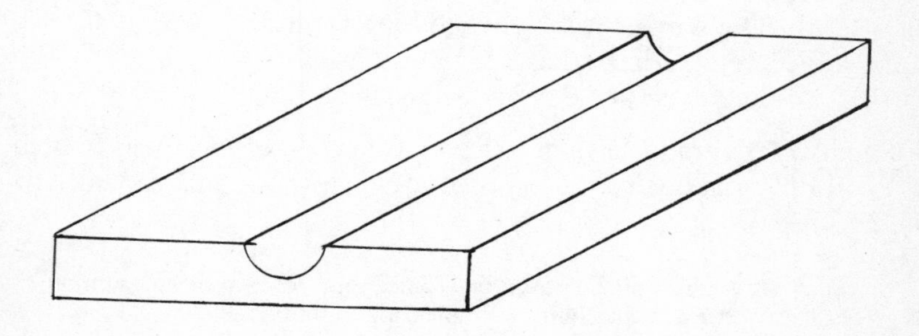

What has been incised into the paving stones of this floor is a

**ROMAN BOARD GAME**

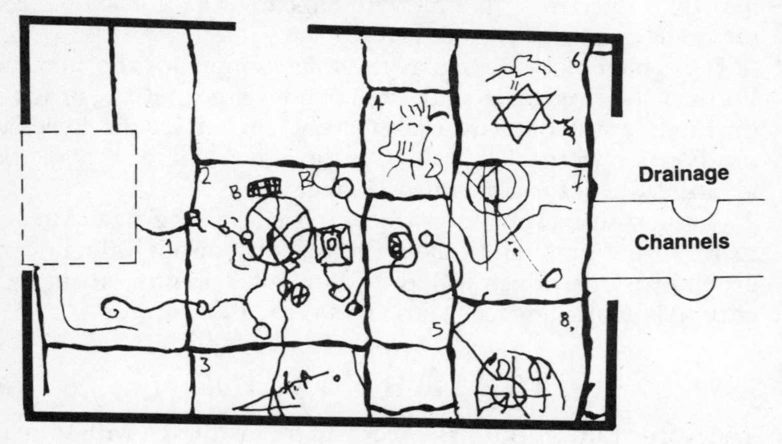


Just as soldiers in every period of history seek to fill their off-duty hours with games, so did the Roman soldiers. Some historians have wondered if these same games in this courtyard are a reminder of the way in which the Roman soldiers treated Jesus. Using the drawing above, locate

## The Game of the King

It has been suggested that the rules of this game may have been as follows:

1. Only condemned prisoners could play.
2. The condemned were made to win.
3. The winner was crowned king for a day.
4. He was dressed as a king and mocked.
5. At the end of the day, they killed him.

Now let's read Matthew's description of how Jesus was treated by the Roman guards after his condemnation by Pilate. Matthew 27:27–29:

> Then the soldiers of the governor [Pilate] tood Jesus into the common hall, and gathered unto him the whole band of soldiers.

> And they stripped him, and put on him a scarlet robe [the color of royalty].
>
> And when they had platted a crown of thorns, they put it upon his head, and a reed in his right hand; and they bowed the knee before him, and mocked him, saying, Hail, King of the Jews.

Actually these games, as we see them today, may be placed in a later period than Jesus' day, but you are free to draw your own conclusions about them.

This is the last stop of today's walk. To leave the Sisters of Sion follow the walkway up to the stairs, and when you reach the exit, you can either turn RIGHT into the bookshop or LEFT and exit to the street.

## SISTERS OF SION BOOKSHOP

The sisters stock a large selection of the most important books on the Holy Land and in many languages as well. Their prices are very fair, and their service is excellent. You can pay for your purchases in either Israeli currency or your own currency. At the rear of this bookshop is the door that leads you back onto the street in front of the Sisters of Sion. The next section tells you how to get back to various parts of the city.

## GETTING BACK TO THE CITY

**Damascus Gate on Foot.** Turn RIGHT, and walk to the end of the road. There turn RIGHT, and in less than fifteen minutes, you will be at the Damascus Gate.

**Dung Gate on Foot.** Turn RIGHT, and walk to the end of the road. There turn LEFT, and in fifteen minutes you will be at the Dung Gate next to the Western Wall of the Temple Mount.

## CONTINUING ON TO THE NEXT WALK

You are only a few steps away. Turn LEFT, and a few yards down the street go UP the ramp with the metal fence, which is located on the opposite side of the street. This is the Al-Omariya Boys' School and located here is the First Station of the Cross.

## VIA DOLOROSA (THE WAY OF THE CROSS)

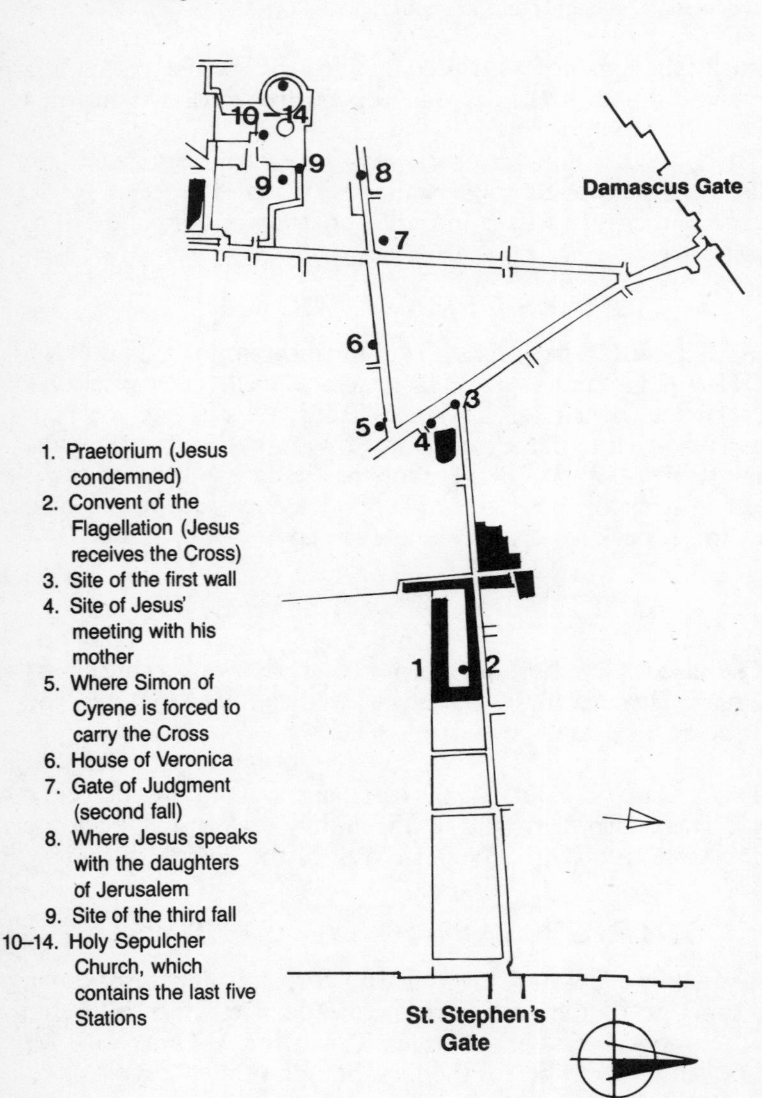

WALK

# 6

## *The Last Day*

| EVENT | SITE |
|---|---|
| • The Journey to Calvary | Via Dolorosa (the Way of the Cross) |
| • The Crucifixion and Burial | Church of the Holy Sepulcher<br>The Garden Tomb |

TODAY'S WALKING ROUTE, THE FOURTEEN STATIONS OF THE CROSS

| STATION | EVENT COMMEMORATED |
|---|---|
| 1. | Jesus is condemned to death. |
| 2. | He receives the Cross. |
| 3. | He falls under the Cross the first time. |
| 4. | Jesus meets his mother, Mary. |
| 5. | Simon of Cyrene carries his Cross. |
| 6. | Veronica wipes his brow. |
| 7. | He falls the second time. |
| 8. | Jesus speaks to the women of Jerusalem. |
| 9. | He falls the third time. |
| 10. | He is stripped of his garments. |
| 11. | He is nailed to the Cross. |
| 12. | He dies on the Cross. |
| 13. | His body is taken down from the Cross. |
| 14. | His body is anointed and laid in the Sepulcher. |

STREET SIGN INDICATING THE WAY OF THE CROSS

Today's tour goal is to follow the traditional path of Jesus on his last day in Jerusalem, beginning at the place of Judgment and ending at Calvary. This journey will take us from the remains of the Antonia Fortress to the Church of the Holy Sepulcher, a route known as the Via Dolorosa ("Sorrowful Way"), the Stations of the Cross, or the Way of the Cross. We will conclude our tour at the Garden Tomb.

To identify each station, the city planners have laid the paving stones in a semicircular pattern in front of each station along the street.

## SPECIAL SUGGESTIONS

- Never go on Sunday. Most churches are closed to visitors, including the Garden Tomb.
- Carry a flashlight or candle with you.
- Carry your Bible with you.

## GETTING TO THE STARTING POINT

Your starting point for today's tour is the Lion's Gate (Saint Stephen's Gate).

**By Taxi.** This is the only tour for which I strongly suggest you take a taxi. No bus comes up close to this gate. It is a short ride from any point in the city.

**By Car.** Leave your car at home, for when you finish your walk today, you will be a long way from where you parked.

**By Foot.** Enter the Damascus Gate and walk straight ahead, bearing LEFT at the first fork in the road at the falafel stand. Continue ahead until you reach Via Dolorosa Street. Turn LEFT, and walk ahead past the Sisters of Sion (which you will recognize from yesterday's walk), and you will see a green fence alongside a ramp across the street. Go up this ramp. This is the starting point today.

**Continuing on from Walk 5.** That's easy. As you emerge from the Sisters of Sion Bookshop, turn LEFT. Across the street, a few feet down the road, is the green railing alongside the ramp. This is the Al-Omariya Boys' School, which is the first stop on today's walk.

## THE STATIONS OF THE CROSS

To quote a respected clergyman who lives in Jerusalem, Father Murphy O'Connor, the Stations are "defined by faith, not by history." The Stations are a religious devotion dating to the Crusader period. It is a way to help Christians identify with the final sufferings of Jesus, a reenactment of the drama. Some of the events of the Via Dolorosa are found in the New Testament, and others were inserted to emphasize New Testament statements. Non-Catholic readers should be aware that all Catholic churches contain Stations of the Cross so that carrying out this devotion is not confined to Jerusalem.

## Is There Another Suggested Route to Calvary?

Yes. Some church historians feel that Jesus may have been taken to Herod's Palace for judgment, which was located at Jaffa Gate. Today the remains are called the Citadel or David's Tower. This raises the historical question of where Pilate was residing.

The evidence indicates that it could have been either the Antonia Fortress or King Herod's Palace. It is logical to believe that Pilate would have chosen to stay in the palace while visiting Jerusalem. (His headquarters were in Caesarea; like Antipas, he was in Jerusalem because of the holiday.) Yet it is just as logical to assume that Pilate would have stayed close to his troops in the Antonia, which Josephus has described as being like a palace. It is hoped that future historians will turn up evidence to solve this riddle.

## Some Highlights Along Today's Walk

- The Suggested Prison of Jesus.
- Ethiopian monks living on the roof of the Holy Sepulcher Church.
- An incredible view of the Old City.
- An ancient cistern where crosses were reported found.
- A rock-cut tomb from Jesus' day.

It is very important that you carry a flashlight or candle.

Enter the Old City through the Lion's Gate (Saint Stephen's Gate). As you pass through the gate, the sign on the RIGHT wall will read "Al Mujahdeen Road." Walk straight ahead, and in about a minute or so you will see a rest area of stone on the LEFT side of this road. Stop here. Walk up to the Orientation Map at the end of this area. From this map, familiarize yourself as to exactly where you are in the Old City, as well as the route we are following today, the Way of the Cross.

When you are ready, please walk straight ahead into the Old City. In less than ten minutes you will be at a green iron railing on the LEFT side and a ramp going up. When you reach the wooden entrance doors to the first Station, a paved courtyard, there will be a watchman there. It is necessary to give him a small tip to enter. In the event that for any reason he won't let you enter, proceed to Station II. Pick up the directions below in the section on Station II.

## STATION I: JESUS IS CONDEMNED AT THE PRAETORIUM

Tradition holds that somewhere in this courtyard Pilate set up his Judgment seat (Gabbatha) and judged Jesus. There was a Crusader church here, but unfortunately it no longer exists today.

Pilate was not convinced that Jesus was guilty of anything, but he had him scourged to placate the Jewish leaders and would then have released him. But they reminded him that Jesus had said he was a king and that such a claim made him an enemy of Tiberius Caesar, the emperor. John 19:12–13:

> If thou let this man go, thou art not Caesar's friend: Whosoever maketh himself a king, speaketh against Caesar.
>
> When Pilate therefore heard that saying, he brought Jesus forth, and sat down in the judgment seat in a place that is called the Pavement but in Hebrew Gabbatha.

**STATION I**

It is important to remember that Jesus was convicted and sentenced to death for sedition against the Roman Empire—for setting up his Kingdom as a rival (so it was seen) to that of the Caesars.

Now walk back in the direction that you just came from, and go up the first staircase on your LEFT. Walk up to the very large window that has a grille over it. Look down. You will have a marvelous view of the Temple Mount. This should give you a realistic feeling of how the Roman soldiers felt, looking down at the Jews on the Mount.

When you are ready, leave through the same doors you entered. We are now heading for Station II.

When you reach the bottom of the exit ramp, make a sharp RIGHT. Walk about twenty-five steps, and on the LEFT is the entrance to the Church of the Flagellation, inside which is located Station II. Enter through the double bronze doors. Take the first LEFT and follow this path to the end, where there is an entrance door on the LEFT. Once inside you are in the Convent of the Flagellation. The convent is open daily in winter, October 1 to March 31, 8 A.M. to noon, 1 to 5 P.M., in summer, April 1 to September 30, 8 A.M. to noon, 2 to 6 P.M.

## STATION II: JESUS RECEIVES THE CROSS.

FLASHLIGHT ON.

The room is dark, so give your eyes a couple of minutes to adjust to the dimness. Please note that the church architecture is Baroque. It is common for Baroque art to be represented by three-dimensional statues, which give a very vivid impression. Now let's study the church art, beginning in the LEFT hand corner and going clockwise.

**Left corner.** Below the word "Lithostrotos" set in the mosaic, we see a pensive Jesus, hands bound, calmly awaiting his fate. Now move along to the

**Painting on the wall.** Pilate, having passed judgment on Jesus, washes his hands of the whole affair. We see Jesus portrayed in a red cloak being led away by his Roman guards, while others are preparing the Cross.

**Left wall.** We see a representation of Jesus receiving the Cross.

STATION II

**Rear wall.** Jesus is depicted in the red cloak. John and Mary Magdalene are seen shielding Jesus' mother, Mary, from seeing his suffering.

**The Striated Paving Stones.** Off to the RIGHT against the wall, you will see more examples of striated paving stones. This tells us that we are still in what was part of the Antonia Fortress. Actually the other side of this wall is the Sisters of Sion, which we visited on the previous walk.

As you leave here, be sure to notice the fine capitals along the path as you exit. Once outside turn RIGHT, and walk along until you reach the second building after the Sisters of Sion. You will recognize it by the double carved wooden doors on the RIGHT. This is

## The Prison of Christ

Although this is not one of the Stations of the Cross, I thought it interesting enough to stop at while you are here. The sign on this church reads, "Greek Orthodox Patriarchate of Jerusalem, Prison of Christ." Visiting hours are 8 A.M. to 5 P.M., closed Sundays.

No one can say for sure if Jesus was indeed held at this site while awaiting the execution of his sentence, but this church is also on the site of the Antonia Fortress.

Once inside go to the LEFT and down to the door at the bottom of the short staircase. In the event the door is locked, go up the staircase and turn LEFT. The door on the end is the residence of the monk who cares for this property. Ring the bell, and he will open the door leading down to the prison for you.

We are going to make two stops here. Please have your flashlight or candle ready. The monk will point out the direction of the first site, which is LEFT as you go in and then straight down the hallway. The entrance to the cave is on the RIGHT.

## The Rock-Cut Cave

Walk inside and keep following the path straight ahead. When you reach what appears to be the last room, turn RIGHT into a room that has a picture behind a window grille. Now notice the stone seat.

As pictured, two holes were cut into the stone to secure the prisoner's legs. His hands were then chained to the notches cut into the ceiling above the seat.

Leaving this place of confinement go back out to the hallway the same way you came in here. Once in the hallway turn LEFT and walk about ten steps, to where you will see an entrance on the LEFT. The monk will turn the lights on for you. However, you will still need your flashlight or candle down below.

Continue all the way to the bottom of the spiral staircase. When you reach the lower level, you are at a site that is known locally as

## The Prison of the Thieves

This large common prison was, as you can see, chiseled out of the bedrock. Walk over to the ledge running around part of the wall. Sit down on it. Now raise both hands over your head. Notice that there are notches cut into the wall above the ledge. This would have been to chain the prisoner's hands. It is certainly a very foreboding place in which to be incarcerated. On the other side of the room is a pit, which may have been used for solitary confinement.

When you are ready to leave, return to the staircase. As you depart, it is customary to leave a small contribution in the box that is provided; the money is used for the maintenance of this site. Now leave this church, and once outside on the street turn RIGHT and continue ahead to the end of the street, where you will now turn LEFT. Walk ahead for a few steps and look down at

## The Roman Paving Stones

As indicated by the sign put up by the Ministry of Tourism, this street may have existed in Jesus' day. You might like to have a picture of yourself standing on these same paving stones. On your LEFT are two columns held together by metal bands. This is the site of

## STATION III: JESUS FALLS THE FIRST TIME.

This property is owned by the Armenian Catholic Patriarchate. To the LEFT above the door is a representation of Jesus falling under the weight of the Cross.

Although the Gospels do not mention the falls, Christian tradition has preserved these events. Since Jesus was scourged prior to being led to Calvary, his condition would have been greatly weakened. One recorded fact does substantiate the probability of Jesus having possibly fallen, for a little way up at Station V, Simon of Cyrene was ordered to carry his Cross.

Do not try to enter the main doors to the RIGHT, as that is where the administrative offices are located. Now walk ahead a few feet, and you will find on the same side of the street

STATION III

## STATION IV: JESUS MEETS HIS MOTHER.

This station is under the care of the Armenian Catholic Church. If you recall at Station II we saw an artistic representation of John and Mary Magdalene shielding Jesus' mother from seeing him being led to the Cross by his Roman guards. This is the event remembered at this Station.

The next Station is just a few feet down the street at the corner. Look for the semicircular paving stones on the street.

## STATION V: SIMON OF CYRENE CARRIES JESUS' CROSS.

You can easily identify this station by the white stone plaque with the crossed hands to the LEFT of the gray-and-silver gates. Simon

STATION IV

STATION V

was a native of Cyrene, a city in North Africa (modern Shahhat, Libya). He was probably on a Passover pilgrimage to Jerusalem. He carried Jesus' Cross the rest of the way to Calvary. Luke 23:26:

> And as they led him away, they laid hold upon one Simon, a Cyrenian, coming out of the country, and on him they laid the cross, that he might bear it after Jesus.

Turn RIGHT and begin walking up the hill. Stop when you come out of the arched (tunnel) roof over the street. Look at the column fitted into the wall on your LEFT between the two arched doorways. This is

## STATION VI: THE HOUSE OF VERONICA.

STATION VI

The traditional story tells of a noble lady who wiped Jesus' face with her veil as he was being led to his Crucifixion; he rewarded her by leaving a picture of his face on the veil. It began as a tradition in the Crusader period. The column you see marks the place of her house.

Now continue up the hill, but before you reach the cross street, I would like to pass on to you a word of caution. You will be entering a bazaar. This indicates narrow streets and huge crowds. Unfortunately bazaars all over the world attract pickpockets. Please be extra careful with your purses and wallets.

The next Station is located directly ahead on the opposite side of the cross street. Since it is usually very crowded there, I suggest you do the reading about this Station from the end of this street.

## STATION VII: JESUS FALLS A SECOND TIME.

Jesus may have exhausted himself coming up the hill that we have just climbed. The column marking this station is on the RIGHT. The mosaic plaque on the wall quotes from John and indicates that Jesus may have been taken outside the walled city at this point to the place of Crucifixion (Calvary, in Hebrew Golgotha). John 19:17:

> And he, bearing his cross went forth into a place called the place of a skull, which is called in the Hebrew Golgotha.

Jewish law of the time forbade executions and burials to take place within the city. Thus at some point Jesus would have been led out through a city gate to meet his fate.

### The Gate of Judgment

Some scholars believe that a gate existed at this spot in Jesus' time, called the Gate of Judgment. The Romans affixed a sign on the gate to indicate why each prisoner had been condemned. If Jesus *was* led out of the city at this point, it would definitely place the Holy Sepulcher outside the city walls in Jesus' time.

Now let's move on to the next station. Turn LEFT if you are facing Station VII, take three steps, and make a sharp RIGHT,

**STATION VII**
(The extra Roman "one" is a design element.)

walking up a hill. A little way up this street on the RIGHT is a bookshop, and opposite it, embedded in the wall, is

## STATION VIII: JESUS SPEAKS TO THE DAUGHTERS OF JERUSALEM.

The base of the column here contains Greek letters, which spell *Nika* ("Victory"). Under Roman law it was strictly forbidden to show any sign of sympathy to a condemned prisoner. Yet the righteous women of Jerusalem did so as Jesus passed by. Luke 23:27–29:

> And there followed him a great company of people, and of women, which also bewailed and lamented him.

**STATION VIII**

> But Jesus turning unto them said, Daughters of Jerusalem, weep not for me, but weep for yourselves, and for your children
>
> For, behold, the days are coming, in which they shall say, Blessed are the barren, and the wombs that never bare, and the paps which never gave suck.

It seems that even in all his agony he was trying to tell these women that Jerusalem would soon be destroyed and their children would be caught up in the destruction.

Jerusalem was destroyed about forty years later, and hundreds of thousands of innocent women and children were indeed caught up in it and starved to death or murdered by the Romans.

When these Stations were established in Crusader times, one could continue directly to the next Station. Today we must follow the modern streets. So, retrace your steps down the hill to the main street and turn RIGHT. In about five minutes you will arrive at a very wide staircase on your RIGHT. The large black sign reads "Coptic Orthodox Patriarchate." Go up this staircase, and once on top, follow the alley to your LEFT. It ends as a church with a column leaning against the wall on the LEFT. This is

## STATION IX: JESUS FALLS A THIRD TIME.

The broken column is all there is to this station. To the LEFT of this column is a wide metal door. Go through it onto the

## Roof of the Holy Sepulcher Church

This edifice, the holiest shrine in Christendom, is open daily from 4:30 A.M. to 7 P.M, in summer to 8 P.M. Modest dress is required at all times.

Living on this roof, in the huts with the green doors, are Ethiopian Coptic monks. They live up here all year round. If they ever leave, they will forfeit their right to the Holy Sepulcher to the other sects who also occupy this most holy church.

Walk over to the

## Dome-Roofed Building in the Center

You are looking at the roof of the Church of Saint Helena. She is associated with the finding of the True Cross. It is very difficult to see through the screened windows; however, a little later we will go below and visit this site.

Now let's visit the Ethiopians' church. If a monk is present, indicate to him that you wish to go below into their church. If he is not available, position yourself as you were when you first entered the roof. Go to the RIGHT hand corner, and enter through the door. It is a low entrance, so please watch your head.

DOME OF CHURCH OF SAINT HELENA

## The Upper Church

This Ethiopian church has two murals. The one on the LEFT represents the Trinity and the painting on the RIGHT shows the

ETHIOPIAN CHAPEL

visit of the Queen of Sheba to King Solomon, when she tested him with perplexing questions.

Now continue down below to the lower church. The light switches are on the RIGHT wall as you are going down the steps. I hope you enjoyed this little side trip, which most visitors to Jerusalem do not get to make. As you exit from this church, you are in the courtyard of the Church of the Holy Sepulcher.

## THE HOLY SEPULCHER

Located inside this church are Stations X through XIV. I suggest that you walk over to a shady spot in this courtyard and read a bit about this site before going inside.

THE STATIONS INSIDE

| STATION | EVENT |
|---|---|
| X | Jesus is stripped of his garments. |
| XI | He is nailed to the Cross. |
| XII | He dies on the Cross. |
| XIII | He is taken down from the Cross. |
| XIV | His body is laid in the sepulcher. |

**COURTYARD OF THE CHURCH OF HOLY SEPULCHER**

This church is, of course, one of the most important Christian shrines in the Holy Land, but it is also one of the most confusing. This is because it has been destroyed and rebuilt many times over the centuries, and six different Christian sects lay claim to it.

I have tried to simplify matters by concentrating primarily on the Five Stations located within it. However, if you have the time, it would repay you to explore this church by yourself.

## Calvary

In the time of Jesus, there was no church, only a bald hill (Golgotha, or in its Latin form, Calvary), with a valley on the LEFT. Now enter the Holy Sepulcher Church. Once inside make a sharp RIGHT hand turn.

## Climbing the Stairs to Golgotha

As you climb the stairway, you are actually climbing the steep hill that existed in Jesus' day. Hold onto the railing and it will be easier to climb up. Make a sharp RIGHT HAND turn and go up the stairs. When you reach the top of the stairs, walk ahead a few feet and stop at the circular design in the mosaic floor. This is where we commemorate Jesus being stripped of his garments.

## STATION X: JESUS IS STRIPPED OF HIS GARMENTS.

Roman law granted soldiers the right to share the clothing of those who were crucified. John 19:23–24:

> Then the soldiers, when they had crucified Jesus, took his garments, and made four parts, to every soldier a part; and also his coat; now the coat was woven without seam, woven from top throughout.

GOLD MOSAIC CEILING

> They said therefore among themselves, let us not rent it, but cast lots for it, whose it shall be: that the scripture might be fulfilled, which saith they parted my raiment among them, and for my vesture they did cast lots. These things therefore the soldiers did.

FLASHLIGHT ON.

Now walk forward toward the altar on the RIGHT hand side of the room. Take a minute to study the magnificent gold mosaic ceiling. The altar in front of you represents

## STATION XI: JESUS IS NAILED TO THE CROSS.

Jesus and the two thieves are crucified. John 19:18:

> Where they crucified him, and two others with him, on either side one, and Jesus in the midst.

STATION XI

**THE CRUCIFIED MAN**

Pilate, who had apparently gone along to oversee things, had a sign made in Hebrew and Greek and Latin and mounted it on the Cross: "Jesus of Nazareth, King of the Jews." Luke 23:38:

> And a superscription also was written over him in letters of Greek, and Latin, and Hebrew, THIS IS THE KING OF THE JEWS:

On crucifixes, this sign is represented by a piece of paper above the figure's head and the initials "INRI," for *Iesus Nazarenus Rex Iudeorum*. When the elders protested to Pilate that it should read that Jesus had merely *said* he was king of the Jews, Pilate refused to alter his words, John 19:22:

> Pilate answered, What I have written I have written.

In 1968, in an area known as French Hill on the outskirts of Jerusalem, a tomb from Jesus' time was discovered. It revealed the only known archaeological evidence yet found of a man who had been crucified. This discovery was important in clarifying many theories regarding the Roman method of crucifixion. Up until this discovery, the standard crucifix showed the body stretched out full length on a tall pole with a cross bar and fastened by nails through the hands and the feet. From the bones found we know that this standard position was incorrect. Here are some facts about the actual procedure in Jesus' day:

• The condemned was usually stripped nude.

• In this area the cross was made from olive wood, that being the most readily available variety. And since the standard olive tree is not tall, we can assume that the cross was short, too, perhaps barely the height of a man.

• Nails were driven through the forearms just above the wrists, not the hands.

• A seat supported the buttocks.

• A spike 7 inches long was driven through a piece of olive wood (to prevent the spike from working its way out) and then driven through the prisoner's heel bones.

Now please cross the room to the second altar. This is

## STATION XII: HE DIES ON THE CROSS

Look down below the altar. The gold disk you see indicates that this was the spot where Jesus' cross stood. The two black circles in the mosaic on either side of the altar toward the rear indicate the places that the crosses of the two thieves stood. Matthew 27:38:

> Then were there two thieves crucified with him: one on the right hand, and another on the left.

Passersby mocked Jesus, as did the Roman soldiers standing by, jeering that he had saved others, why couldn't he save himself. Mark 15:29–30, Luke 23:36–37:

> And they that passed by railed on him, wagging their heads, and saying, Ah, thou that detroyest the temple, and buildest it in three days. Save thyself, and come down from the cross.
>
> And the soldiers also mocked him, coming to him, and offering him vinegar.
>
> And saying, If thou be king of the Jews, save thyself.

Jesus resigned the care of his mother to his disciple and prepared to die. John 19:28:

SITE
OF THE
CRUXIFIXION

After this, Jesus, knowing that all things were now accomplished, that the scripture might be fulfilled, saith, I thirst.

Instead of water, the soldiers gave him vinegar and hyssop, a bitter herb, and he prepared to die. Matthew 27:50:

Jesus, when he had cried again with a loud voice, yielded up the ghost.

From noon until midafternoon there was "darkness over the whole land." Then Jesus cried out for the last time. Mark 15:34:

And at the ninth hour Jesus cried with a loud voice saying, Eloi, Eloi, lama sabachthani? Which is, being interpreted, My God, My God, why has thou forsaken me?

The Holy Land was occasionally visited by earthquake, and one seemed to have occurred at the moment Jesus died. Matthew 27:51:

> And, behold, the vail of the temple was rent in twain, from the top to the bottom: and the earth did quake, and the rocks rent.

Look down to the RIGHT of the altar. The vertical split in the rock you see marks the place of the earthquake.

The Roman soldiers were suddenly frightened by what they had done. Mark 15:39.

> And when the centurion, which stood over against him, saw that he so cried out, and gave up the Ghost, he said, Truly this man was the Son of God.

Now move to the center where you will see a glass-enclosed statue between the two altars. This is

## STATION XIII: JESUS' BODY IS TAKEN DOWN FROM THE CROSS

This Station is called the Grief of Mary, or in Latin, *Mater Dolorosa* ("Sorrowful Mother"). Mary witnessed his death. John 19:25:

> Now there stood by the cross of Jesus his mother.

To hasten the death of those being crucified, it was the custom of the times to break the prisoner's legs with a mallet. This would permit the blood to flow faster, and the prisoner would die from internal bleeding. However, this was not done to Jesus since he appeared to be dead already. John 19:32–34:

> Then came the soldiers, and brake the legs of the first, and of the other which was crucified with him.
>
> But when they came to Jesus, and saw that he was dead already, they brake not his legs:
>
> But one of the soldiers with a spear pierced his side, and forthwith came there out blood and water.

At this point Joseph of Arimathea, a righteous member of the Sanhedrin, went to Pilate and begged for the body of Jesus so that he might have a proper burial. Luke 23:52:

THE MATER DOLOROSA

This man went to Pilate, and begged the body of Jesus.

Now turn around and head for the staircase leading down below which is on your RIGHT hand side, at the end of the room. Please hold on to the railing going down, for the steps are very steep and usually slippery.

At the bottom of the stairs, turn LEFT and walk over to the flat stone slab, above which are suspended eight white lamps.

## The Stone of the Anointing

This stone, which the architects of today's church placed between Golgotha and the Tomb, commemorates the preparation of Jesus' body before it was placed in the newly cut tomb.

After Pilate released Jesus' body, Joseph prepared it for burial as was the custom of the time. John 19:40:

STONE OF THE ANOINTING

> Then they took the body of Jesus, and wound it in linen clothes with the spices as the manner of the Jews is to bury.

Now retrace your steps, pass the stairway you just came down, and continue until you reach a lighted glass window, behind which you see bedrock. This is part of the Hill of Golgotha.

Now please turn LEFT and continue down the hallway for about twenty-five steps until you reach the next stairway leading down below, where we will visit

## The Armenian Chapel

Before going down the steps I want you to notice the crosses incised into the stones. Pilgrims over the centuries have left a remembrance of their visit to this chapel.

Once at the bottom of the stairs study the mosaic floor, such a work of love and art. Please do NOT walk on the mosaic. The pictures you see laid into this floor are of early Armenian churches.

THE ARMENIAN CHAPEL

## The Chapel of Saint Helena

This chapel is dedicated to Helena, mother of Emperor Constantine the Great. You will recall that, when we stood on the roof of the Holy Sepulcher, we looked through screened windows and couldn't see much below. Now we are standing in the area below.

It was through his mother's influence that Constantine built the greatest churches of the times: the church of the Holy Sepulcher, the Church of the Nativity in Bethlehem, and the Eleona Church which we visited on an earlier Walk. However, history has chiefly associated Helena with the finding of what was believed to be

## The True Cross

This tradition is remembered in the area down below and to the RIGHT of where you are now. Go down the few steps, and you will be standing in an ancient rock-cut cistern. This is where we commemorate the tradition of the finding of the True Cross. This chapel is named the Church of the Holy Cross or the Church of Saint Helena.

Now leave this area as you entered by reclimbing the steps. Once back above in the hallway, turn RIGHT, and continue along this corridor. As you walk along, notice the amount of restoration work being done. At the end of the corridor, you will be standing in

## The Rotunda

The structure in the center of this room houses the traditional tomb of Jesus, which is also

## STATION XIV: JESUS IS BURIED.

The proof that this area did indeed have tombs from Jesus' time will be evident in a minute when we visit the remains of such a tomb located in

## The Syrian Chapel

FLASHLIGHT ON

Walk around the rotunda, bearing to your RIGHT. You will pass a wall with two huge Crusader columns and then one with three columns. After the last column on this wall, turn RIGHT into the Syrian Chapel. Once inside this chapel, enter the opening in the rock on the LEFT side of the room.

### A Word of Caution

DO NOT ENTER THIS TOMB WITHOUT A LIGHT. It's very dangerous. There is a deep pit on the LEFT as you enter. So please stay to the RIGHT at all times while inside the Tomb.

SEPULCHER OF JOSEPH OF ARIMATHEA

This chapel is commonly known as the Sepulcher of Joseph of Arimathea. Joseph was a Pharisee and possibly a secret disciple of Jesus, who had recently cut a new tomb in the rock of his garden. The Scriptures tell us that, once he received Jesus' body from Pilate, he buried it in his own new tomb. Matthew 27:59–60:

> And when Joseph had taken the body, he wrapped it in a clean linen cloth,
>
> And laid it in his own tomb, which he had hewn out in the rock: and he rolled a great stone to the door of the sepulcher, and departed.

The tomb you just visited is a traditional tomb from Jesus' time. Now please return to the rotunda, walking around and entering the structure in the center of the room from the side opposite the Syrian Chapel.

The first room you enter is called

## The Chapel of the Angel

The stone represents the place where the angel sat at the time of Jesus' Resurrection.

## The Holy Sepulcher

The inner room, according to tradition, is the place where Jesus' body was laid by Joseph. The slab of stone marks the spot where the tomb stood.

We have now completed our visit inside this church. But I ask you: *Please don't end your tour here*. However tired you may be by this time, I urge you to continue on to the Garden Tomb. It is peaceful and beautifully laid out, an ideal place to remember Jesus.

**THE HOLY SEPULCHER**

## THE GARDEN TOMB

Exit from the main doors of the Church of the Holy Sepulcher, located just past the Stone of the Anointing. Once outside in the courtyard, walk ahead and turn LEFT onto the street. You will pass the Church of the Redeemer on the RIGHT and then come to an intersection. Turn LEFT and you are heading for the Damascus Gate. (This is the street we came up a little while ago when we were on our way to the Holy Sepulcher Church.) Go out the Damascus Gate, up to the street level. Cross the street, and walk over to the sign that reads "Schmidt's Girls' College." Continue up this street, heading away from the Damascus Gate, and about three quarters of the way down the street you will see on your RIGHT the entrance to the Garden Tomb.

The Garden Tomb is considered by many Christians to be the true site of Calvary (Golgotha). It was suggested as an alternative site by the German scholar Otto Thenius in 1840. In the late 1800s General "Chinese" Gordon put forth a theory regarding this site, which we will discuss in a few minutes. As I have stressed throughout all these Walks, it is not necessary to play historical geography; what happened is more important than where it actually happened.

THE GARDEN TOMB

## The Setting

The Garden is open 8 A.M. to noon and 2:30 to 5 P.M. Closed on Sundays. Prayer services are held here in English every Sunday at 9 A.M., after which it is closed to visitors for the rest of the day.

It is a lovely place. One gets a feeling of reverence and wants to linger on a while and read from the Scriptures. There are many quiet spots with benches here in the garden, for just that purpose. After entering through the bookshop, turn RIGHT and follow the arrows leading to Skull Hill. On the RIGHT are rest rooms as well as a cold water fountain. At the end of the path is a platform leading up to

## Skull Hill

Read the sign, which quotes from John 19:16–18, relating the story of Jesus being taken to Golgotha (Skull Hill).

## General Gordon's Theory

Gordon, on an extended visit to the Holy Land, lodged in the large building across the main road and just inside the Old City walls of today. He had a vision of the skeletal body of Jesus being stretched out over the entire city—the feet down in the City of David and the skull on this hill. Just off to the LEFT of where you are now standing, there are two depressions cut into the mountain. Gordon identified these depressions as eye sockets and the rest of the mountain as Jesus' skull. (Thus the name "Skull Hill.")

Scientific investigation has proved these depressions to be rock-cut cisterns. Be that as it may, we are deeply indebted to General Gordon for today's beautiful Garden Tomb site. Although the archaeological evidence does not support the claims of this site as the tomb of Jesus, it has, nonetheless, won acceptance among thousands of Christians.

## The Rags in the Trees

Look at the trees on the very top of the hill. They usually have rags hanging from the branches. During the Muslim holy days of Ramadan, custom calls for a cannon, located on this hill, to be fired. Instead of bullets, it is stuffed with rags, and some of the rags become caught in the branches. There is also a Muslim cemetery there.

Now please go back down the path you just came up, and continue on until you reach the fork and then bear to your RIGHT. Take the first path to the RIGHT. A little way down this graveled path, you will see a grating at ground level. To the LEFT of this is

## A Cistern

Look down through the small opening. It is really difficult to judge the huge size of this cistern, but it is one of the largest ever discovered in Jerusalem. Its liquid capacity is 200,000 gallons. A few years ago they wanted to empty it and called in the local fire brigade. It took five days to pump out the water.

This cistern, especially of such a huge size, is evidence that an irrigation system for a very large garden existed here. We have dated this cistern from the time of Jesus. This cistern may have been used as a place of refuge by early Christians. This is evident from the two crosses that were incised into the plaster, dating to the Byzantine period. Continue down the path. When you are down below, walk to the opening in the rock on the RIGHT.

THE GREAT CISTERN

## The Tomb

There are several points of interest inside the Tomb. This is a rock-cut tomb from First Temple times (eight or nine hundred years B.C.). It is one in a series of tombs cut into the ridge of this mountain, all predating Jesus. As you walk inside, please be careful, since the step is high. Watch your head.

**The Weeping Chamber.** The first room you enter is the room where friends and families of the deceased would gather to mourn, upon a visit to this tomb. Look through the bars at the RIGHT hand side of the room.

**Crosses on wall.** Although you can only make out one cross today, two such crosses were found here when the tomb was first discovered. The second one has faded from the exposure to light. These symbols clearly indicate that these tombs were used by early Christians during the Byzantine period.

**Burial Niches, left side.** The rock has been cut away leaving a "pillow" rest for the head of the deceased as well as a resting place for his feet. The "pillow" seems to have been a custom from Old Testament times onward.

**Burial Niche, center.** An unfinished adult resting place.

**Burial Niche, right side.** An unfinished adult resting place. Leaving this tomb, please duck your head. Walk across the patio, and on the RIGHT hand side note

## The Ossuary

At the Church of Dominus Flevit, you saw many ossuaries. With your finger trace the two circular designs incised into this ossuary. The design is called a rosette. It is a circle with petals arranged in rows of three, six, nine, or twelve petals. This particular ossuary has a six-petal design. The second thing to look at here is located just to the LEFT of the Ossuary:

## A Round Stone Door

If you remember, on the Walk in Bethpage, we saw a tomb that had been sealed with a large stone. Now you can have a good close-up view of such a stone. This type of tomb closure, which was to prevent animals from eating the corpses, was used during the time of the Second Temple. The New Testament is very clear that Jesus' tomb was likewise sealed.

Leaving here, go up the staircase on your RIGHT. As you are walking up, notice the sign at the bottom of the stairs. It quotes from John 19:40–42 and relates the events dealing with the burial of Jesus. At the top of the staircase, cross over to what appears to be a sunken garden, which is straight ahead and to the LEFT. This is actually the remains of

## The Wine Press

This is the final evidence that we are in an area of what once was a garden. Look at this press carefully. Notice that a sort of drainage channel emerges from the rock. This indicates that there is more to the press than is currently visible to our eye. The grapes were probably crushed farther back, and the liquid was allowed to drain into the drainage basins you see down below.

DRAINAGE CHANNEL FROM WINE PRESS

## GETTING BACK TO THE CITY

**To West Jerusalem.** Opposite the Garden Tomb is the East Jerusalem Bus Terminal. Take bus No. 27 to Jaffa Road. Alternatively, when you leave the Garden Tomb, you can turn RIGHT and walk into West Jerusalem, a twenty-minute walk, all up a steep hill.

**By Foot to East Jerusalem.** Leaving the Garden Tomb, turn LEFT. At the end of this street is the main street of East Jerusalem, Nablus Road.

Well, that concludes our sixth and last walk. I hope that I have achieved my goal of sharing with you most of the possible, and many of the probable, places that Jesus is reported to have visited in the New Testament. Likewise that I have successfully recreated the times in which Jesus lived.

If you wish to stay here in the Garden Tomb a while longer, please do. There are many lovely little private places in which you can meditate.

I thank you very much for having allowed me to share this experience with you. This is what comes for those of us who live here in our Magic City of Jerusalem.

Shalom,
I. Martin

# CHRISTIAN GUESTHOUSES AND HOSTELS IN JERUSALEM

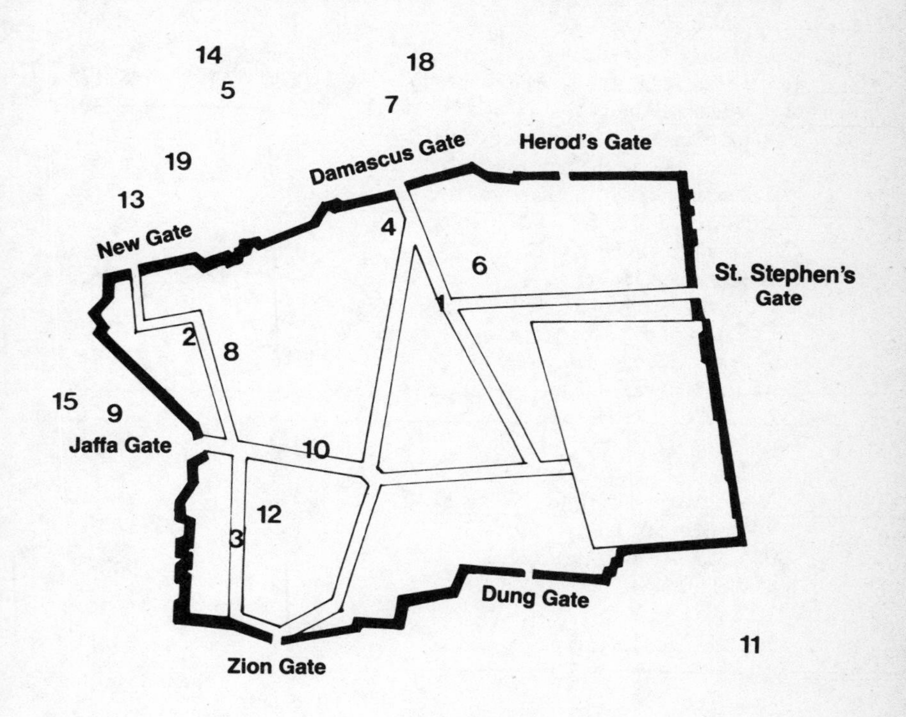


| NAME | P.O.B. | | TELEPHONE |
|---|---|---|---|
| 1. Armenian Catholic Patriarchate 3rd Station Via Dolorosa | 19546 | D | 284262 |
| 2. Casa Nova, Casa Nova Road, Old City | 1321 | | 282791 |
| 3. Christ Church Hostel, Jaffa Gate | 14037 | D | 282082 |
| 4. Dom Polski, Christian Quarter | 20256 | | 282017 |
| 5. Dom Polski, HaShlishit Street, 8 | 277 | D | 285916 |

| NAME | P.O.B. | | TELEPHONE |
|---|---|---|---|
| 6. Ecce Homo Convent, Sisters of Sion 2nd Station Via Dolorosa | 19056 | D-G | 282445 |
| 7. Franciscans of Mary, White Sisters Nablus Road, 9 | 19049 | D-G | 282633 |
| 8. Greek Catholic Patriarchate Jaffa Gate, Old City | 14130 | | 282023 271968/9 |
| 9. Lazarist Convent, Agron Street, 20 | 1144 | | 227530 |
| 10. Lutheran Hostel, St. Mark's Road | 14051 | D | 282120 |
| 11. Maison d'Abraham for pilgrims and students by special application to the director | 19680 | D | 284591 |
| 12. Maronite Convent, Maronite Street, 25 | 14219 | | 282158 |
| 13. Notre Dame of Jerusalem Center opposite the New Gate | 20531 | | 289723 |
| 14. Rumanian Hostel Shivtei Israel Street, 46 | | D | 287355 |
| 15. Sisters of the Rosary, Agron Street, 14 | 54 | | 228529 |
| 16. Saint Andrew's Hospice near Railway Station | 14216 | | 717701 |
| 17. Saint Charles Hospice, German Colony Lloyd-George Street, 12 | 8020 | | 637737 |
| 18. Saint Georges Hostel, Nablus Road | 19018 | | 283302 |
| 19. Salesian Sisters, Ayin Het, 18 | 159 | | 287567 |
| 20. Y.M.C.A. Aelia Capitolina Nablus Road, 29 | | | 282375 |
| 21. Y.W.C.A., Wadi Joz | | | 282593 |
| 22. Y.M.C.A., King David Street, 26 | | | 227111 |

# Index